PATRIOTIC INGENUOUSNESS

JULEON SCHINS

Patriotic Ingenuousness

© 2019 Juleon M. Schins. All rights reserved.

No part of this publication may be reproduced, stored in a retrieval system or transmitted in any way by any means, electronic, mechanical, photocopy, recording or otherwise without the prior permission of the author except as provided by US copyright law.

ISBN 978-1-64550-499-3 (Paperback)

CONTENTS

This book is part of a 2019 decalogue consisting of

- Sign of Times: Music Anthology and Lyric Analysis
- Hollywood Misogyny
- Beginners' Guide to the FED:
  Why it is Unique on our Planet
- The Kennedy Kurse: Four Obvious Konnektions
- Manichaeism and Satanic Child Abuse
- Progressive Intolerance: Last Stop Before Hitler
- Patriotic Ingenuousness
- Deism versus Theism:
  2-7 in the Scientific Arena of the 20th Century
- Feminine Feminist:
  A Missing Link Eluding Discovery
- The Snake: Three Millennia of Anti-Semitism

Dedicated to the
virtue of patriotism

Introduction
A New Era

Historians, physicists, and archeologists divide the past into ages or eras: physicists talk in billions of years, archeologists in millions of years, and historians in centuries. In this book we take the perspective of an historian. After the era of Empires (Persian, Assyrian, Ancient Greek, Ancient Roman), characterized by god-like emperors, came the Christian Medieval era, characterized by divinely appointed Kings. Outside Christianity most cultures were either tribal or continued like ancient empires. Christian supremacy ended with the French Revolution, making place for Illumination and Nationalism. After the Middle Ages Europe appeared as the mightiest culture: not only in the technological sense, but also in the moral sense. Illumination claims these features for herself, considering the Christian Medieval era as backward and "dark", but they simply got their calculation totally wrong. While all non-Christian cultures were stuck in slavery and total lack of technological advance,[1] Europe made a definitive end to slavery, invented the chimney, the windmill, the two-axed front wheel of a carriage, the artistic renaissance and

1 think of the way in which the pyramids were built

gothic churches[2]. These feats took the Christians about ten centuries. The comes Illumination, it destroys France's most beautiful cathedrals, re-introduces slavery in order to make money on African people, and claims the values of liberty, fraternity, and equality are their invention? This is a joke.

Were it not that, even today, most people on our planet believe the story. Just take a look at the America's: in the North all natives have either been killed, or thrown into ghetto's they call "native reserves". On the other hand, in the South (that is, from Mexico through Argentina) all degrees of racial mixtures can be found. Too bad Illumination turned South-America into a chaos by funding all terrorist groups popping up there, and by granting a steady supply of drugs for a sick society. Illumination is the display window of a dirty money launderer! I cannot find any kinder way to put it. After the quite short supernova of Illumination, many other revolutions came. The difference with all previous eras, is that Illumination and the following revolutions *persisted*, instead of being *replaced*. Thus came the oligarchies, the industrial revolution, the financial revolution, the democracies, the computational revolution, and the information revolution.

It took humanity three thousand years to realize that democracies are the most dangerous of all. Nothing is wrong with the concept, of course. The problem is human

2 Apart from a few roman basilicas, the only churches visited to date because of their imposing beauty

nature. Only the ingenuous believe that human nature is "clean". Only the ingenuous believe that a man come to power will not be morally affected by that power. By the way, in this booklet the terms "ingenuousness" and "naivety" are interchangeable, as are "natural" and "physical" law.

The main proposal brought forward in this book is that a new "age" has come to fullness: the era in which mafia's, freemasons, and all kind of deep state organizations, have reached budgets comparable to or much bigger than National Products, thereby reducing democracies to Muppet shows. In two-party democracies, enmity between the two parties is fueled and financed by the deep state.

In other words, it does not mind any more who are the visible faces constituting your government, as they are nothing but mercenaries for invisible mafia's standing like huge giants behind them. The British people had their Monarchy, which ended with the increasing power of the Houses of Parliament. You had your Democracies, of whom the right honorable Margaret Baroness Hilda Thatcher, LG, OM, DStJ, PC, FRS, HonFRSC was the last presentable species.

Please allow a physicists his nerd's remark: this historical era has some similitude with a black hole. Nothing happens in there, except an extremely slow burn-down, until a huge explosion occurs, on whose combustion products neighboring black holes will once feed.

Unless.

Unless we, the ordinary, more or less "good" or "good-willing" people, unite and throw the deep state out. That is much easier than you think. Just have a look at what the Icelanders did when the deep state urged for higher taxes. They simply put some judges and bankers behind bars, and that was it.

Rothschild wrote in his yearly report of 2016 (the year of the Brexit-referendum) that the British decision meant a big blow for western economic advancement. Read carefully what he writes. Also carefully read the Washington Post and the New York Times. They are but a single voice, Rothschild's. His mafia, which is called "EZ" in this booklet, owns America, Europe, and significant parts of Africa,[3] Australia, and Russia.[4]

As a rule, for better legibility, **all quoted passages are written using a different font** as compared to the standard.

---

3 Everything except Chinese properties, I guess, though I have not studied China at all, and I could not possibly tell to what extent it already is EZ-penetrated.

4 But how can this be, as America and Russia are enemies for life? Just remember what I wrote, a few lines higher up, concerning the two-party system in the United States, and EZ obviously always representing the leftist "ideal". And remember that Mr. Lenin was put on a heavily guarded train from Switzerland to Russia, in order to overthrow the Tsar and introduce Bolshevism. Stalin had the honor to eliminate all Tsarist forces in the country.

CHAPTER 1
Personal Ingenuousness

This chapter presents examples of widely accepted personal ingenuousness. Since it is always easiest to recognize vices in other people than in oneself, we start out by discussing the easiest and best-known subspecies of ingenuousness, the "personal" one of teenage girls (boys of that age are even more ingenuous, but girls pay the bill, and that is more visible than the boys' psychic pain).[5]

---

5 This is why so many girls love the lyrics of Bruce Springsteen ("now I act as if I don't remember, and she acts like she don't care; but I remember us driving with my brother's car...") or REM ("Everybody Hurts" describes a boy's feelings of suicide, no doubt due to his having lost his girl). On the podium of Glastonbury, live in 2003, he sank to his knees when the lyrics told him to. The girls all went crazy (in the good sense of the word).

1.1 Ingenuousness of the Girl

Open door: most girls are most beautiful from their 16th to their 26th. Another open door: many psycho's are willing to use force, even on girls between their 12th and their 16th. A third open door: the large majority of fathers is physically unable to talk about sexual psycho's with their 12 year old girls. A fourth open door: parents have increasingly less time to spend on their children due to the EZ parasite that squeezes them like oranges. Conclusion: the percentage of stolen, violated, or murdered girls between 6 and 16 is rising in the US.[6] I do not invite you to look up the statistics. They make one vomit.

1.1.1 Mechanism of propagation

The natural process that warrants the propagation of this kind of girlish ingenuousness and parental educational inability contains at least these elements:

6 The same holds for boys, obviously.

- *Parents like to leave in inheritance to their progeny a good, attractive and just world.*
- *They avoid talking to their children about atrocities and injustices, in order not to hurt them psychologically.*
- *It is always difficult to admit that the world is much worse than it seems, even more so to the extent that we share the guilt.*
- *It is more comfortable to believe all the trash fed to us by the media, than to painfully evaluate, time and again, the trustworthiness of the sources.*[7]

1.1.2 Possible remedies

Girls between 12 and 15 who show off their corporal beauty have no idea *at all* of the enormous strength of sexual attraction they generate in 30+ aged men (among whom myself). Moreover, they have no idea of what type of boys of their age (for whom they clothe like that) they attract. And if they happen to attract a fine teenager, they have no idea of how to cope with sexual advances. They

---

7 The reader might ask, "Even in the case of high-reputation broadcasting companies like BBC?" Yes, even then. Chapter 4 gives a convincing example of how BBC structurally lied and deceived, and still lie and deceive, in order to protect an immoral source they were morally compelled to reveal. The highest directives have an assassin mentality.

just want to be able to tell their girlfriends that they lost that heavy burden called virginity,[8] and how good it felt.[9] Parents who do not see the suicidal aspect of such behavior, are so dumb they'd better stop reading this book. As for those who do see it, but lack the confidence of their own children ("ah, you know, puberty..." is the usual excuse), apparently lack the courage to explain to their daughters the difference between "being desired for one's potential to satisfy sexually" and "to be loved". Or that "making love" is as nonsensical a notion as "making faith". If parents are unable to help their children in the most difficult time of their youth, how are these poor kids supposed to find out? When a girl returns home crying, because her boyfriend left her when she told him she wanted the baby; when she was raped or because she feels as such; it is... too late. The girl paid too high a price for her ingenuousness, and the parents will have to live with their ugly consciences.

It is better to prevent than console. For smart girls a sincere and personal talk with either parent will do the job. Twelve-year old girls that are more intuitive probably need something blunter, like watching "The Ugly Truth" (starring Gerald Butler and Katherine Heigl) with daddy. Daddy's task is to interrupt the movie every five minutes, and explain what exactly excites men sexually in the scenes; and to comment explicitly that a woman's humiliation and submissive pain amplify the feeling of

---

8 Heavy burden? Sure. That is exactly the way EZ is destroying Christian values.

9 In most cases a pain lie.

sexual excitation in *all* males. The element of pain is particularly revealing — it smells of the devil. Hence, it should not come as a surprise that practical materialism, which ignores spirituality in humans, is destroying 2000 years of healthy Catholic sexual doctrine. This materialism is funded by EZ, *which is wise enough to never allow girls of their own bloodline to depart an inch from the Catholic sexual doctrine.* Get it?

1.2 Ingenuousness of the Clergy

This section treats two examples of clerical ingenuousness: one from Rome, the other from Turin.[10]

1.2.1 Father Antonio Ferrua S.I.

Pius XII ordered an archaeological excavation in 1940, with the end of disclosing Peter's tomb underneath the principal altar of St. Peter's Basilica. Due to the German occupation, they had to work secretly. Had the Germans found out, they certainly would have taken control of the project. The Nazis were interested in all means of power, be they technological or mental. The excavations concluded in 1949. Pius XII publicly announced, through

10 The author in no way intends to typify Italy as a country where such ingenuousness is likely to occur. Moreover, the first example is taken from WWII, which was a time in which objective thinking was objectively harder than in times of peace.

a radio message on Christmas 1950, that researchers had found the tomb of St. Peter a few meters right below the principal altar of the basilica, exactly in line with the oral and written tradition.

Margherita Guarducci, Italian archaeologist and professor of Epigraphy, testifies:

> "The actual altar (of Clement VIII, dating from 1594) is built on top of that of Calisto II (1123); that was on its turn built around the altar of Gregory the Great (590-604); this last one was built on top of the so-called "monument of Constantine" (312-326) which contains the first monument of Peter, even older, which goes back to the second century. (...) Inside Peter's monument is found part of a small building attached to a certain red wall which was the background of the first monument of Peter. In the interior of the building there is a wall filled with graffiti (...) dating before Constantine's monument (...). The density of graffiti on the wall testifies to the devotion of the faithful. The first monument of St. Peter has a lid on the floor, covering an ancient tomb (...)".

In 1952 Guarducci asked and obtained permission by Pius XII to study the graffiti, because she had discovered an inaccuracy in an archaeological publication by Antonio Ferrua, S.I. Guarducci directly started to look for the rock with the graffiti 'ΠΕΤΡΟΣ ΕΝΙ' (Peter is inside here). She did not find it anywhere. What could have happened to that enormously important rock?

Father Ferrua thought he'd better take it home.

According to the multi-secular tradition of the Church, St. Peter's bones were located in the tomb under the lid. Why did Ferrua and his team of archaeologists fail to find them?

Under the pounding of the 'cartoccia', Peter's tomb, which initially contained only his bones, soon filled up with debris.

Due to pure incompetence: they used a rough instrument, called 'cartoccia' in Italian, which is similar to a tool for making cylindrical holes in hard soil, for the purpose of planting upright poles. To get to St. Peter's tomb without too much circumvention, *the excavators simply crashed Calisto II's altar.*

Having reached the designated spot, to their surprise the excavators only found their own debris. What did they expect? An angel perhaps, pointing out a golden, nicely polished Arch-of-the-Covenant kind of object?

Anyway, *they gathered the debris for later disposal and continued their search in nearby sites.* Monseigneur Ludwig Kaas, the supervisor responsible for the excavation (who did not trust his four brutes very much), had the habit of inspecting all their debris at the end of the day. He also did so in this occasion, together with the "sanpietrino" (helper in the basilica) Giovanni Segoni.

One of the two noticed something protruding from the debris, which looked like a human bone. Out of mere reverence for the dead, they collected all bones in the debris, catalogued and archived them as originating from the so-called G-wall.[11] Neither Monseigneur Kaas nor Segoni had the slightest idea of having found the remains of St. Peter. Ten years later, when taking a coffee with Segoni, Guarducci interrogated him for the umpteenth time about those inspections with Mgr. Kaas. He faintly remembered having once archived something from the G-Wall. Hearing that and running to the archives was a single thing for Guarducci.

---

11 Wikipedia recounts the conclusions of the Italian anthropologist, Dr. Venerando Correnti:

- The bones of the animal (a mouse that did not find a way out of the tomb) are practically clean compared to human remains, because they were covered with dirt that was later analyzed and found to be from the open and empty tomb which was identified as St. Peter's tomb (because of the inscription 'ΠΕΤΡΟΣ ΕΝΙ', notes the author). On the other hand, all the other tombs next to this finding have a different type of dirt (in addition to inscriptions of the kind "Peter, pray for us, who are buried next to your body".).
- The bones have a reddish color. This is probably due to a purple cloth wrapped around them. The remains of gold thread confirm that these were the bones of some venerated person. It is possible that the early Christians took St. Peter's bones from the original tomb to 'store' them in the niche so they would be kept safe, for the niche was intact starting from the time of Constantine until the findings.
- The bones found here belong to single person: strong, male, of advanced age (around seventy years old), and from the first century.

A year later (1968) Pope Paul VI had to declare that Guarducci had found the bones of St. Peter, exactly under the main altar of St. Peter's Basilica. Guarducci was not a particularly malleable woman: she reprimanded the Pope severely when he had taken part of St. Peter's relics to his private room.

1.2.2 Cardinal Anastasio Alberto Ballestrero

The second example of personal ingenuousness of Catholic clergymen concerns Cardinal Anastasio Alberto Ballestrero O.C.D., archbishop of Turin and pontifical guardian of the shroud. Catholic researchers often come up with endless stories concerning the effect of contaminations, masterpieces of ingenuousness. Is it really so difficult to imagine that Michael Tite cheated? After all, he was the only and exclusive supervisor.[12] Moreover, he had publicly declared his personal conviction that the shroud was a fake *before knowing a thing about laboratory results!* The exact procedure of Tite's fraud, nothing more refined than the Piltdown fraud, was laid bare by Bruno Bonnet-Eymard, who showed convincingly, among many other points, that:

12 This is contradicted by Stephen Jones. His blog is interesting because it contains most of the relevant bibliography: http://theshroudofturin.blogspot.nl/2014/05/my-theory-that-radiocarbon-dating_30.html

- *The sample sizes as taken from the shroud by Franco Testore and Gabriel Vial did not match the sample sizes delivered to the three laboratories.*[13]
- *Michael Tite took over from Teddy Hall when he retired and after some anonymous businessman donated 1 million pounds for an ostensible proof of the Shroud being a fake.*[14]
- *The protocol provided in filming every single second of the 20-hour procedure... somehow the crucial part showing Tite putting the samples into the containers got lost.*
- *Nobody seems to know who decided, against protocol, to expel Madame Mechtilde Flury-Lemberg, of the Abegg-Stiftung in Berne. Her high qualifications and insisting presence probably did not please Tite too much.*
- *Although Tite did not need any arrangements with the laboratory scientists,*[15] *Bonnet-Eymard's research shows he had arrangements with both the*

---

13 https://www.ewtn.com/library/issues/sturp.txt

14 See Joe Marino on https://shroudstory.com/2013/05/10/comment-promoted-do-not-blindly-accept-the-results-of-the-1988-dating/

15 Douglas Donahue and Paul Damon from Tucson, Arizona; Willy Wölfli from Zürich; Edward (Teddy) Hall and Robert Hedges from Oxford. All three laboratories are specialized in Accelerator Mass Spectrometry, the standard technique used to identify the "mass over charge ratio" of the molecular ions emitted from the sample.

American (Donahue and Damon) and English labs (Hall and Hedges).[16]

- *Tite asked Jacques Évin (from the Radio Carbon lab at Villeurbanne, France) to address the Musée de Cluny for medieval samples "of the same fabric as the Turin shroud" but his request was refused. On specific request of Tite, Évin stole a few tufts of thread from the cope of Saint Louis d'Anjou (1274-1297), and had Gabriel Vial confirm that the texture of the cloth was "similar in every point to that of the Holy Shroud". Still a third time, Tite himself requested such texture from Ian Wilson of the British Society for the Turin Shroud.*

My best guess is that Tite lit his cigars with the shroud samples. Would you not do the same, if driven by his publicly declared intentions? Tite misled Cardinal Ballestrero[17] so easily, that the latter —saintly priest or not— entered and left history as a sad example of staggering ingenuousness.

16 See Bruno Bonnet-Eymard on http://crc-internet.org/our-doctrine/catholic-counter-reformation/holy-shroud-turin/ii-conclusion-new-trial/

17 As far as the author knows, Ballestrero failed to check the Pope's command, by means of the May 1987 letter from the loggia-P2 freemason Cardinal Agostino Casaroli, then Secretary of State of the Vatican, to leave all supervision in the hands of Michael Tite and Luigi Gonella. Even if it were the Pope's command, he should not have obeyed it without previously asking for the Pope's reasons.

1.3 Ingenuousness of the Show Star

Why would an extremely attractive woman, with a splendid voice like Whitney Houston, filled to the brim of cocaine and countless other drugs, drown in her bath in 2012? Somehow her family managed to keep her out of the list of celebrity suicides, as published by Wikipedia.[18] Why would other beautiful people, with at her feet at least a thousand adorers per toe, suicide? Check the photos of British actress and model Lucy Gordon (2009) and Jiah Khan (2013). The same holds for attractive men: David Carradine (2009) and humorist Robin Williams (2014). My own guess is that these people, apart from possibly Robin Williams, who suffered a severe mental illness, have a completely unrealistic image of our world, themselves included. Why is suicidality so much higher among stars (whether sportive or entertainment) than among ordinary people? The answer is quite simple: stars are pushed, to the point of abuse, since their tender youth (Michael Jackson) to exhibit their special talent. Parents do so with the good intention to "help their kids reach national VIP status" but are so ingenuous that they do not realize their behavior is mere selfishness. *"I think she gets it from me"*, (Dirty Dancing, Baby's mother to her annoyed friend).

---

18 https://en.wikipedia.org/wiki/Whitney_Houston
https://en.wikipedia.org/wiki/List_of_suicides
https://en.wikipedia.org/wiki/List_of_suicides_in_the_21st_century

CHAPTER 2
Professional Ingenuousness

After having discussed some examples of the subspecies "personal ingenuousness" we now move on to a second subspecies, that of "professional ingenuousness". This chapter focuses specifically on ingenuousness among professionals in the field of *natural philosophy*. In the following, the adjective *natural* is sometimes omitted but always implicit unless explicitly said otherwise.

I regret to say this so crudely, as a physicist to philosophers, but the fact is that *extremely* little of what philosophers have said in history, still stands today. The reason is simple: philosophy is a more difficult discipline than natural science. Some philosopher might object: "But all scientific advances are possible only by means of logic, and that is a philosophical discipline". I do not compart this view. Logic is not a philosophical prerogative. Mathematicians and taxi drivers can claim it just as well.

2.1 Natural Philosophy and Sciences

Generally feared is Stephen Hawking's thesis: 'philosophy is dead'. Although I agree with Hawking's reasoning, I do not endorse his conclusion. The reason for this nuance (between the conclusion and the reasons leading to it) is in the definition of the term 'philosophy'. For Hawking, philosophy is nothing more than an 'ancilla scientiae' (slave of science), since according to him matter is the only thing that exists; a rather outdated materialism typical of determinists in the wake of Albert Einstein. As explained in full detail in the appendices, such materialism is incompatible with natural science; hence, it is a mere loss of time to study Hawking's concept of philosophy.

Physical discovery has always preceded philosophical thinking. This was already plain even before the "official" birth of physics in the case of momentum conservation discovered by two great 14th century scientists: Buridan[19]

19 Jean Buridan (1295 – 1363) was a French priest who sowed the seeds of the Copernican revolution in Europe. He developed the concept of impetus, the first step toward the modern concept of inertia, and an important development in the history of medieval science. His name is most familiar through the thought experiment known as Buridan's ass (a thought experiment that does not appear in his extant writings). Born, most probably, in Béthune, France, Buridan studied and later taught at the University of Paris. Unusually, he spent his academic life in the faculty of arts, rather than obtaining the doctorate in Theology that typically prepared the way for a career in Philosophy. He further maintained his intellectual independence by remaining a secular clerk, rather than joining a religious Order. By 1340, his confidence had grown sufficiently for him to launch an attack on his predecessor, William of Ockham. Buridan also wrote on solutions to paradoxes such as the liar paradox. An ordinance of Louis XI, in 1473, directed against the nominalists, prohibited the reading of his works. The bishop Albert of Saxony, himself renowned as a logician, was among the most notable of his students.

and Oresme.[20] The more science consolidated the higher the frequency of such examples, like

- *the inexistence of the electrodynamic ether in the XIX century;*
- *the existence of a quantum-mechanical wave function for every possible physical system, in the XX century, as well as*
- *the spatio-temporal relativity of Einstein.*

In all these cases, the role of philosophy has been to hamper physical progress due to the philosophers' anti-reactionary clinging, first to Aristotle and Plato, and later to Kant.

20 Nicole Oresme was born around 1320 near Caen, Normandy. The fact that Oresme attended the royally sponsored and subsidized College of Navarre, an institution for students too poor to pay their expenses while studying at the University of Paris, makes it probable that he came from a peasant family. Oresme studied arts in Paris, together with Jean Buridan (the so-called founder of the French school of natural philosophy), Albert of Saxony and perhaps Marsilius of Inghen, and there received the Magister Artium. He was already a regent master in arts by 1342, during the crisis over William of Ockham's natural philosophy. In 1348, he was a student of theology in Paris. In 1356, he received his doctorate and in the same year, he became grand master (grand-maître) of the College of Navarre. Around 1369, he began a series of translations of Aristotelian works at the request of Charles V, into the French language rather than the (at that time) more popular Latin. Oresme's works have been published much more in Britain than in France (exception made for the great Pierre Duhem), because Oresme defended the continuity across the middle Ages and Modernity.

There simply exists no single historical example of scientific advance made possible or even encouraged by natural philosophy. Quite the contrary, examples abound in which philosophers joined all forces to consider physical models as describing 'human-built pictures of reality', instead of reality itself. I again regret to say so, but from the XIV century onward, Aristotelianism has been structurally retrograde in its natural philosophical teachings. It easily survived Buridan and Oresme. It even managed to put Galilei's writings on the index in the XVII century, that is, twenty-one centuries after the Master (Aristotle) himself! The catholic *index librorum prohibitorum* did not excel in authority, given that all Italian universities immediately took up teaching Galilei's theories — thereby introducing bitter fights among the professors.

Philosophers tend to think *a priori*, while natural scientists think *a posteriori*: they observe, define their quantities, and if possible, a crucial experiment. Eventually they come up with a mathematical model that roughly describes the results. The model keeps being refined with every bit of new experimental evidence.[21] For a natural scientist, this is the meaning of 'understanding nature', and that is where the natural philosopher's task should begin. Thinking *a priori* is a contradiction in terms, as far as I am concerned. I'm not surprised that more than 90% of philosophical writings through the ages

21 This is an extremely ambiguous statement. An unambiguous formulation requires the concept of 'limit', explained in appendix A1.3.

are nonsensical. Remember the infamous case of Alan Sokal, who wrote a fake article in 1996, called "Transgressing the Boundaries: Toward a Transformative Hermeneutics of Quantum Gravity" for the Journal "Social Text".[22] This was no doubt a heavy blow for sociology and linguistics, the survivors among whom are still busy licking their wounds.

No doubt, Aristotle is the greatest philosopher of all times. However, his major contribution to philosophy is not in the field of natural philosophy (philosophy of nature), but in metaphysics. His discovery goes by the name of 'hylemorphism', which describes how an object can change either with or without losing its identity. The third and fourth appendices give specific examples of novel applications of Aristotle's hylemorphism. After Aristotle's finding, (which was a clear example of *a posteriori* philosophy, as nobody could possibly come up with such a model without having studied natural behavior before), the history of philosophy only came up with utterly crazy, though widely appreciated, ideas: Descartes, Hegel, Kant, Schopenhauer, and an infinite list of nuts.

2.2 Creationism

Most popular attacks on the Christian faith come from renowned scientists like Daniel Wegner, Daniel Dennett, Ian Glynn, Edward Wilson, Richard Dawkins, and

---

22 46–47: 217–252. doi:10.2307/466856

Stephen Hawking. To these attacks, Christian philosophers usually respond with philosophical arguments. To a scientist, however, their arguments are circular.[23]

The 'strong' creationism idea teaches that God created the earth six thousand years ago, because that is what the Old Testament describes, when one interprets the ages and the relation of kinship literally. They have no problem in declaring that God created its paleontological sites and fossils all along. There is no way to prove them wrong. Theoretically, it is equally possible that God created the world yesterday and in doing so, he filled our minds with the pertinent memories. Another option is that there is no material world at all, but everybody dreams.

Science is not about gathering all options that *could have occurred*, but selecting that only option *which is the most likely to have occurred, assuming that God does not fool us*. Strong creationism is incompatible with this view on science. Strong creationists seem to revel in apparent contradictions, the more the better.

---

23 As an example, consider the XX century Christian philosophers' arguments against evolution: it would imply the possibility of the simple to give birth to the complex, without sufficient cause. Scientists consider the first organic cell as a genetic program. Depending on the circumstances (the input) all types of output are possible, even an evolutionary path toward the human body. Did the complex proceed from the simple without a cause? No, the evolutionary path toward the human body was partly contained in the genetic information of the first cell, and partly in the surroundings. To scientists the philosopher's conclusion was already included in their premises, i.e., circular.

'Weak' creationism accepts the scientifically established ages of the universe (around 13.7 billion years) and of the earth (around 4.5 billion years), but it dogmatically refuses to accept the evolution of species. For them the stability of species is a perpetual miracle.

2.3 Intelligent Design versus Retrograde Evolutionism

Christian philosophers are not particularly fond of scientists taking a philosophical stance. In the case of Michael Behe this antagonism is ludicrous, as no scientist hurt materialism so badly in the XXIst century as did Michael Behe. Some Christian philosophers even manage to confuse Behe's Intelligent Design with creationism, thereby showing that they do not understand the first thing of it.

Michael Behe wrote his challenging book *Darwin's Black Box* in 1996. He unmasked the nonsense propagated by many well-known evolutionists, the worst example being Richard Dawkins' phased-evolution model, as explained later in this section. Behe also defends the impossibility to explain, based on only Darwinist principles (variation and selection), the evolution of whatever biological structure or process, with bacterial flagella, cilia, the blood coagulation cascade, the immune system, and vesicular traffic as highlights.[24]

He bases his argument on the novel concept of 'irreducible complexity'. I do not believe today's scientific knowledge allows for a full-fledged definition of this concept. Behe did the best he could: The complexity of an object with a certain function is irreducible when it becomes dysfunctional upon modifying whatever part.

This is quite impressive, already. But a full comprehension requires more biochemical knowledge of the birth of new species. And all we have today, are but phantasies of evolutionists, who think that by juxtaposing similar molecules, they solve the scientific problem.

Behe makes it clear that the Darwinist principles (variation and selection) only operate on biological constructs that already carry out a function. This sounds like "bursting through an open door" (Dutchism), I know, but quite clearly the evolutionary community still badly needs someone to tell them.

Do not get me wrong: I am not at all saying here that Darwinist principles (variation and selection) are erroneous. They are perfectly valid and there are many nice examples proving their validity (see appendix A2.2). What Behe says, and every sensible scientist with him, is that the Darwinist principles can only *modify* existing species, not *generate them.*

---

24 In his 'On the origin of species' Darwin already confessed having no idea how his theory could ever explain the evolution of an organ as complex as the eye. He was more clear-sighted than his followers were.

Evolutionists thought they knew better. Toward the end of the 20th century, Dawkins was convinced he could mitigate the exuberant statistical improbabilities, always claimed by statistical physicists, by subdividing the evolutionary problem into distinct 'phases'.

If the gene carrying the essential information for an evolutionary leap would have to change on 120 sites (refer to appendix A2.2 for the biological terminology), Dawkins would define 120 'phases': one phase for each genetic mutation. If each variation affected all 120 sites with equal probability (the Christian scientists' supposition), the probability of making the evolutionary leap is one in 4^{120} per mutation. If mutations occur at a rate of one per second, the leap would require an average waiting time of 4^{120} seconds, which is of the order of 10^{65} years. For the leap to occur once in the full lifetime of our planet (4.5 billion years), one needs a constant population of 10^{55} individuals. *The earth does not even contain that number of atoms*, let alone individuals of a biological species!

Therefore, Dawkins proposed his famous *Ansatz*: *mutations only affect those sites that do not yet coincide with the required one*. In this case, a similar calculation yields an evolutionary time of just a few minutes, rather than 10^{65} years. Behe correctly pointed out that Dawkins' theory is blatantly creationist, as it supposes an intelligent being that determines at every moment which sites may and which may not mutate. Dawkins' model denies the very foundation of Darwinism! Dawkins failed to realize that his model needs a God-like final cause, directing evolution toward a goal established outside material reality. Dawkins was supposed to be one of the smarter evolutionists. Imagine what kind of nonsense the less gifted evolutionists were preaching!

Funny, is it not? When Dawkins launches an openly creationist theory, nobody stirs, apart from a single unknown biochemist. However, when that very single unknown biochemist proposes an interesting new concept (irreducible complexity), fully compatible with the Darwinian mechanisms of variation and selection (and with a Christian view of the world), evolutionists collectively turn furious, dubbing him a creationist (which in science is the same as calling someone an SOB.[25]

25 Too bad a choir of retarded Christian philosophers joins the critics.

Did this cilium rotor develop by chance? Biologists emphatically confirm. Mathematicians emphatically deny.[26] *To me personally, it looks too much like a designed object. After hundreds of thousands of years of humanity, our very best engineers were able to produce a dynamo. Yet, when left alone, it rots away pitifully.*

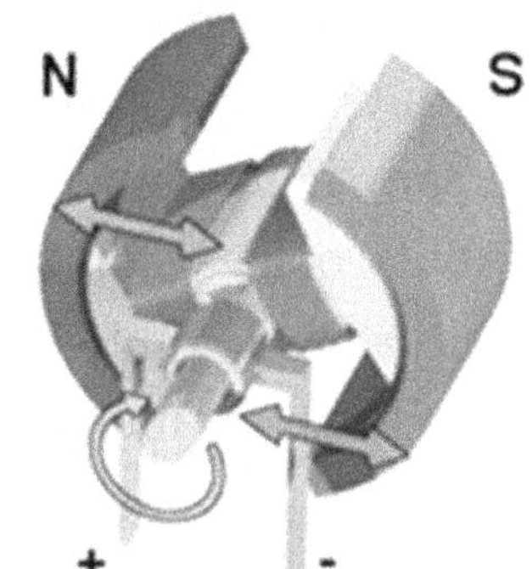

2.4 Entropy According to Penrose

It is an irony of history that Dawkins' creationist model is one of the three essential ingredients for a Christian explanation of the creation of man. Dawkins' somewhat limited library needs some extension, however, with two more notions: quantum mechanics and entropy.

Sir Roger Penrose elegantly treats the notion of entropy in his classical book *The Emperor's New Mind.* He calculates e.g. the enormous ratio between the "initial entropy" (at the moment of the Big Bang), and the entropy of our present universe. This ratio is so fantastic that

26 Too bad for the biologists, it is the mathematicians' job to *calculate*, not theirs, as they have not the faintest idea about numbers higher than 1000.

Penrose chose to illustrate the Big Bang with a magician swinging his wand, short of an explicit religious confession.

The smaller the initial entropy, the larger is the amount of macroscopically different final states. A room uniformly filled with air has a very high entropy, and very little can change: opening a door would cause pressure variations of less than 0.01%, an explosion slightly more. The situation is quite different if the room was initially void, with all air molecules concentrated in a light bulb. In this case, the initial entropy is very small. Many final states can occur, due to the explosion of the bulb, which scatters pieces of glass of different sizes all over the place.

An analogous argument holds for our universe, with gravity providing the main difference: due to gravity black holes have a much smaller entropy than a same-size universe uniformly filled with the same amount of matter. In the end, all universes, with or without life, die an “entropic” death: an ever expanding collection of black holes in which nothing happens anymore.

2.5 Bell’s Inequalities

The third ingredient for a Christian explanation of the evolution of humankind (if your memory fails you: the first one was Dawkins’ wrong theory, and the second one was entropy) is given by quantum mechanics, and more specifically, by the monumental discovery by John Bell. He wrote down a provocatively simple inequality in 1964.

Scientists soon christened it "Bell's inequality", and shortly thereafter, "Bell inequality": omitting the "s" allowed the use of this expression as an adjective, like in "Bell-inequality experiments". Appendix A3 provides some more information on these inequalities. For the purpose of this chapter, it is not necessary to know what they are. The reader only needs to know that since October 2015,[27] it is definitively established that

Quantum Choices ***Cannot Possibly*** *Issue From Matter*

In simpler words: every single quantum event reveals the choice of a spiritual being. If materialism was already a dead philosophical model because of the existence of universal laws (appendix A1), it is now stone-dead (appendix A3). In the context of Penrose's entropy, this means that our universe required a huge amount of quantum decisions (by a non-material entity that will be called God for simplicity, although reality is more complex[28]) to arrive at its present situation.

27 Hanson published a loophole-free Bell experiment (see appendix A3).

28 This is a reference to the existence of Angels, on one hand, and to the fact that the Christian view is not pantheistic; that is to say, the world would differ very little from God's *longa manus* if apart from creating it he also took all decisions.

2.6 Directed Evolution

The section title is just another word for 13.7 billion years of divine quantum choices. A combination of the notions of Behe, Penrose, Bell, and Dawkins, provides a model for the creation of man, which is compatible with both the Catholic Magisterium and recent scientific insight (quantum mechanics, ordinary statistics, and gravity). Traditional Christians should conform to the evolution of the human body, along a sequence of fantastic creatures, last of which is our common ancestor with the chimpanzee. They should equally conform to the fact that the fertilized human ovum (egg cell) is nothing but an animal, until God wishes to breathe the human spirit into it. That is to say, there is not even the slightest philosophical difference between Adam's or Eve's creation, and yours or mine. We all started out as animals, and remained so until God chose to "blow His Spirit[29] into that animal". Nobody, no scientist, not even the Holy Roman Catholic Church in all its infallibility, can ever predict at what moment God decides to breathe the human spirit into a fertilized human ovum: the beginning of spirited human life will always be an explicitly divine, unique, personal, irrevocable and unrepeatable act of creation. We humans should consider this as an honor:

29 This process of "blowing the Spirit" belongs intrinsically to the natural state of mankind. It must not be confused with Pentecost, which, although a process of "blowing the Spirit" as well, belongs to the supernatural level: the level of spiritual childhood of God.

clearly, God does not treat us like serial numbers, but just as caringly as he would have treated a single human person.[30] The material aspect of the human body may have evolved along a pre-established plan, subject to the laws of nature, but the human spirit comes to being by an explicit action of God.

The evolution of all species, including humankind, is the result of a series of 'directed events' (quantum elections) in space and time; all of this without the least contradiction with physical laws. Consequently, the tiniest error in quantum choice would have resulted in a universe without biology.

The only way to confute this 'Weltanschauung' consists in finding life elsewhere in our universe. Until today, our radios only detect background noise, driving our friends, the ideological listeners, totally nuts. Extra-terrestrial life may never make it beyond fiction movies. If the author of this book is right, humanity will never find life elsewhere in the universe: neither because of a philosophical impossibility, nor because of a physical one, but because of God's Providence.

30 Some people, believers or not, have a hard time (especially after being told how big the universe is, with plenty of stars so far away that they are already long extinguished by the time their light reaches our planet), imagining this whole universe is there for us only. *Modice fidei!*

2.7 Hume's Guillotine

David Hume was a Scottish philosopher from the 18th century. In his book 'A Treatise of Human Nature' he graciously complains "that his colleagues tend to start their papers in a descriptive and deductive way, up to a certain point; then, almost imperceptibly, the verb 'is' disappears, and instead the verb 'ought' appears in its place." A 20th century philosopher, George Moore, coined the concept 'naturalistic fallacy' to indicate the impossibility of even defining moral categories. Although both of them commit tend to oversimplify (see appendix A5.1), Hume was right in his critique of Christian philosophers.

Hume's guillotine is the elimination of 'is-ought' errors. An 'is-ought' error is the illicit identification of natural properties with moral properties; in simpler words, the illicit substitution of the verb 'is' with the verb 'ought to be'. An example of an 'is-ought' error would be to consider every religion good. This is an instance of a more general philosophical error, in which 'act' is mistaken for 'potency', or spirit for matter. In this section, we will apply Hume's guillotine to two quite similar concepts: to democracy and to democratic laws.

A democracy is established when an independent country decides that their governors be freely elected in an electoral campaign with more than a single political party, by popular vote, counting each vote equally. We do not mean to give a full-blown definition of democracy, but rather to highlight the absence of any moral notion. Many

Christian writers agree theoretically, but in practice, the realization of democracy implies morality. Instead, there should be no difference whatsoever between democracy and tyranny of the majority. The application of Hume's guillotine to the concept of 'democracy' (literally 'power to the people' in Greek) has the following consequences:

- *democracy has nothing to do with morality; there can exist and there have existed moral and immoral democracies; the same goes for monarchies;*
- *the responsibility of granting freedom and tranquility in society is not inherent in the concept of democracy, but it is derived from the concept of morality.*
- *whoever thinks that democracy grants morality more than other political systems, has not read history. E.g., Hitler had a democratic mandate.*

In practice, it is impossible to measure the morality of a society's government: we would have to sum up all of the injustices suffered by each citizen at the hand of civil or military authorities and at the hand of other citizens. There is no other option than to look for indicators of morality of a government. *We argue here that the most efficient indicator of morality of a government is economic growth, because economic growth requires all citizens to exercise human virtues at all levels;* rich and poor, high dignitaries and modest employees. The economy is like a clockwork process in which all parts are optimally integrated. Of course, the morality of the people is to be distinguished from that of the government. If the government is corrupt, there will be little if any economic growth, however virtuous the ordinary people. Hence, the indicator of economic growth does not represent the average morality of the people, but that of the government, or better said, that of the people taking the important decisions.

Naturally, economic growth is not an indicator of instantaneous morality of a government, but of that over a certain past. Sometimes it takes much time for governmental decisions to affect the economy. Below follow three examples of economic consequences of immoral decisions.

- *Chinese communism fixed the maximum of one child per couple. This measure powerfully pushes economic growth at short term (specifically when a monetary fine is due for a second child): it eliminates the poor, rural population (the principle defiler of their statistics) and it encourages the growth of the population in rich areas. Unfortunately, the Chinese ideologists did not foresee the nasty consequence of their immoral law: that the poor preferably aborted their females! The social disaster is indescribable and the pernicious economic consequences are unavoidable. Chinese stocks will fall, and their prisons will burst due to angry young men.*

- *In Greece they had it all, great thinkers like Aristotle and Plato, cultural treasures (Romans loved Greek art) as well as natural ones (beaches, mountains, valleys); but a long tradition of corruption has led the country to the border of bankruptcy. As long as the high political dignitaries are corrupt, nothing will ever change; to the contrary, the more money Europe invests in them, the more corruption will prosper.*
- *Germany, the impressive economic engine of Europe, pays the bill of their anti-nuclear phobia. It is mere irrational sentiment, comparable with the fear of 19th century English farmers who saw a monster on metallic wheels in their fields, driving the livestock mad (bitter milk, spooky creatures, and very mean spirits) with its sounds and smoke plumes; a monster that those crazy city folks call 'train'. As long as Germans do not start to reason, they will keep losing economic strength. The same holds for my own country, The Netherlands.*

Another example typical example of the 'is-ought' error is that of the Christian lawyers who believe that the goal of human laws is safeguarding morality. This is obviously false. Such objects already exist: divine laws, such as Moses' Ten Commandments. Similarly, some Christian lawyers claim that the goal of imprisonment is punishment. This is equally false. The institute inflicting punishment already exists: purgatory (for the lucky ones). These are two examples of philosophically illicit 'divinization' of earthly stuff. 'Divinization' here means the act of attributing supernatural properties (divine punishment, divine law) to merely natural concepts (prison, human law). Let Hume's guillotine squeak! The summary below is an excellent introduction to the next section.

- *The primary goal of human laws is to safeguard liberty and tranquility in society.*
- *The direct goal of prison is twofold: to temporally prepare benevolent convicts for their re-insertion into society, and to definitively isolate malevolent convicts from society, albeit in harsh circumstances. This harshness should not depend on human thoughts of punishment, but EXCLUSIVELY on what society can bear in terms of financial costs.*
- *The goal of a sentence is not punishment, but avoidance of vengeance, and re-establishment of commutative justice as fast and as far as possible.*
- *Punishment is God's prerogative alone. Neither humans, nor human society, should EVER punish for the purpose of serving justice.*

2.8 Legislative Divinization

The principal cause of unjust occidental laws is the ingenuousness of the legislator. As mentioned in the previous section, Christian lawyers tend towards divinizing law. If in some cases the public is angered due to an unjust verdict, those lawyers would say that the ordinary public is not aware of the complexity and intricacy of law.

Laws are there for humans, and not the other way around; if this already applies to divine law, how much more should it apply to human law? An angered society is an unequivocal sign that something is wrong: not necessarily the law itself. Its enforcement can also fail. In any case, blaming the public's ignorance reveals one's failure to grasp the essential: laws are the means for securing tranquility in society. Even though the law might be good in terms of someone's ideas about divine morality, if its implementation provokes social unrest, it is a bad law. *This means by definition that good laws must be different in different countries.*

In my country, it happens regularly that the public reacts indignantly with respect to a verdict. In 2014, an armed robbery took place in a jewelry store in a cozy Dutch town called Deurne. When the wife noticed on the video that two armed men were threatening her husband in the store, she took her car right away to the jewelry store and killed both of the assailants that had the husband at gunpoint. What do the mentally retarded officials from the Dutch public ministry do? They require 200 hours of task punishment plus half a year of conditional imprisonment *for the husband because he had no license for his store-gun.* The poor man decided to buy that gun after suffering a previous armed robbery, which happened four years earlier. Probably needless to say, such an infringement of the law is bingo for the insurance companies.

Examples like this abound in other countries. For example, the state prosecution in Jacksonville, Florida, which threatened Marissa Alexander (34 years old) with 60 years of prison for having fired a warning shot in her own house to end the harassment by her ex-husband. Under the threat of the prosecution, Alexander chose to admit to three charges of aggression, which yielded her 20 years of imprisonment. To defend herself against the prosecution's injustice, Alexander only had to call her two sons to testify — something she chose not to do because the prosecution would have torn them (and whatever little was left of the family bonds) apart in the court of law. The court sentenced Alexander according to the agreement and she went to prison. Strong civic pressure realized her release, three years of prison later. Congratulations, mister ex-husband, you managed to destroy her life and that of her children, too.

On the other hand mister ex-husband, still shuddering all over his body from Alexander's warning shot, did not feel the least restraint in having his 15-year old son testify in court. The boy declared that 'his life changed the day that his step-mother shot a weapon in his presence'. He did not say that 'he had the scare of his life' but 'that his life changed'; it is not difficult to imagine mister ex's lawyers training the boy's answering. The 15-year-old ended his declaration with a sentence straight from university text books: “I was not physically hurt, but I was emotionally and mentally injured.” Ever heard a fifteen-year old speak like that? The most convincing argument against the lack of justice in criminal law is the great difference between states. In the United States, self-defense against the intruder differs from the ‘castle doctrine’ at one end of the spectrum, ‘stand your ground’ half way, and the ‘duty of retreat’ at the other end. In the first case, there is no need to assess the intruder’s intentions, nor of the lethality of his arms. In the second case, the owner has the right to keep his position using a proportional amount of self-defense, which does imply the duty to assess the fighting ability of the intruder. In the third case, there is an obligation to retreat. I do not know for sure which of these is the most just – what I do know is that all three cannot be just, for being incompatible. Every state has its own characteristics, I know, but with respect to nocturnal intrusion, there is no difference at all, yet the laws go all over the place.

CHAPTER 3
Institutional Ingenuousness

The chapter is not too cohesive, as it gathers different examples of institutional ingenuousness, mostly of the legislative kind. The last section about media monopolization (3.7) is important for understanding chapter 4, the only chapter dealing with the novel phenomenon of "collective ingenuousness". The present chapter opens with a concise history of penal law, as most of the legislative ingenuousness occurs on the field of penal laws (3.1). Then we consider the rather self-destructive (from the point of view of the whole society) aspect of most European laws (certainly the Dutch ones) that they encourage nocturnal intrusion by thieves in search for money and high-value small volume items, like electronic gadgets and jewelry (3.2). Section 3.3 shows how to apply Hume's Guillotine to retrograde laws of self-defense. Section 3.4 considers how Christians should deal with ethically wrong laws. Section 3.5 discusses the roots of female discrimination. It is one of the three crucial ingredients of an efficient recipe for collective suicide. The other two are faithlessness and wealth. Peter Schrag, author of "The decline of the WASP" (1971), recognized some of these ingredients, although he seems concerned primarily with the Jewish-WASP power balance in US society.

Since I sympathize with people of all beliefs, including non-believers, I propose a law that counters both female discrimination and its consequence in rich countries, collective suicide. Section 3.6 discusses the medieval US penitentiary regime, and presents the results of applying Hume's Guillotine.

3.1 Talion and Composition

The ancient Jews did not have the slightest inconvenience in determining the measure of mending in case of deliberately inflicted damage: "an eye for an eye, a tooth for a tooth", says the Talion (Ex 21:24). Historically, this law put an end to hereditary resentments, whenever the "Composition" had failed: the private payment of a sum of money agreed upon by the aggressor and the victim or the victim's family.

The Talion consists in making the delinquent suffer what his victim suffered. The Talion is the first historical form of punishment that assumes the existence of a public power that applies a material equivalent between the damage suffered by the victim and the damage inflicted by the aggressor. The Talion succeeds in preventing vengeance, but fails in compensating the victim.

The Composition is an indexation of the harm done, attributing a price to every crime. Germanic tribes of the XII century used the term 'wergild' (from the Latin 'vir', man, and the Saxon 'gild', money) for the price of a homicide. Among the Alemannic tribes, the female wergild was twice the male's (assuming equal social rank). For the Saxons it was the other way around, more in line with contemporaneity. They were quite ahead of their times, these Alemannic tribes!

The distinction between public delicts (crimes) and private ones was already known among the Romans in the V century B.C., and written down in "the laws of the XII Tables" (also called "of roman equality", or "decemviral") and contained norms regulating daily life of the roman people. The state persecuted crimes, while civilians dealt with delicts. During the Roman Republic and Empire, the public domain gradually took over the private domain.

During the early Middle Ages (centuries V through XI), the three sources of law (roman, feudal, and Canon) mixed to some degree. The concepts 'delict' and 'sin' were interchangeable, as were 'punishment' and 'liberation'. The rise of monarchies in the X century characterizes the end of the early Middle Ages. The rediscovery of Roman law had to wait until the XII century. It was the main subject at several universities, initially mostly Italian, along with Germanic and Canon law. In the following centuries (XIII through XVI), private retaliation was not tolerated any more, and lawyers generally agreed on the fact that the goal of punishment is intimidation and discouragement. They introduced different degrees of juridical imputation: for the fool, the furious, the youngsters etc. The XVII century is associated with the far too flattering name 'enlightenment': lawyers like Beccaria and Montesquieu introduced a series of penal reforms, humanizing the punishments, ending torture, introducing equality before the law and the principle of legality, as well as proportionality between delict and punishment. The Italian positivism introduces a new concept in the XVIII century: punishment is determined by the probability of recidivism (Lombroso, Ferri), rather than by the act. In the XIX century, Neo-Kantianism criticizes positivism for lacking a solid scientific base.

In the course of penal history, the goal of punishment has gradually shifted from a religious (punishing) to a consequentialist (anti-idealist) perspective. I embrace the anti-idealist perspective, because all idealisms I know of from universal history, only meant trouble and misery, no matter how noble the ideals. I propose that society use punishment only with an eye on protecting liberty and tranquility. Although the application of justice is a very grateful collateral effect of defending tranquility in society, it may never replace the goal. An important advantage of this perspective is that it facilitates cooperation with people of different beliefs and moral systems, both in the cases of political minority and majority.

3.2 Nocturnal Intrusion Encouraged by Dutch Law

The criminal laws of a country are too important to leave them to historic arbitrariness, or to the free discretion of lawyers not specifically selected for the job. Laws require interdisciplinary, profound, quantitative studies of all relevant correlations. Let us present a simple example. How many instances does the reader of my book know of silent nocturnal intrusions by a tourist asking for directions? Yes indeed, silent nocturnal intrusions are practically always malevolent. More than a waste of time, it is rather a plain injustice to demand from the proprietor whatever verifications concerning the intruder. In my country, intruders who feel the host did not offer sufficient courtesy, sometimes win their case. Hume would turn around in his grave, puking his last reserves.

Some three thousand years ago, the Ancient Jews already used the diurnal criterion as a decisive circumstance. Exodus makes it clear that whoever kills a nocturnal intruder is not guilty of murder: this sounds much like the "castle doctrine" mentioned in section 2.4. The first verses of Exodus, chapter 22 read,

> "If the thief is caught while breaking in and is struck so that he dies, there will be no blood-guiltiness on his account. But if the sun has risen on him, there will be blood-guiltiness on his account. He shall surely make restitution; if he owns nothing, then he shall be sold for his theft."

I do not at all propose to base a modern juridical system on Exodus, certainly not the selling part. But for the self-conceited Christian it is important to remember that when Jesus said that he did not come to abolish law, but to fulfil it (Mt 5:17-19), he was most specifically referring to the Ten Commandments and a little less specifically to the four legislative chapters (20-23) of Exodus. Yet it is understandable that Christians are somewhat puzzled by the enormous differences between the new and old laws.

The difference between the New and Old Testament is that the Old one emphasizes the Infinite Divine Justice and Mercy, while the New one the Infinite Divine Charity; but the New Law by no means replaces the Old Law ("not even a jota shall be changed") because God is Infinitely Just, Merciful, and Loving at the time.

Jesus proclaimed that whoever gets his right cheek slapped should present his left. Does Jesus' new law contradict the old law, which encourages one to throw out the nightly intruder with violence? Of course not! What would Jesus want a poor family father to do, when his exuberantly rich neighbor requires his only sheep? To offer his only ox as well, and resign to contemplating a slow hunger death of wife and children?

The solution is quite simple. Christians *are required* to apply the Old Law whenever rights are trodden of otherwise defenseless people. When it comes to one's own rights, one has the choice to apply the Old Law, and stay put in the love of God, or to apply the New Law, and grow in charity.

Excuse me for digressing.

In the case of noisy nocturnal intrusions, the great majority of the cases concern drunken friends. How many cases do my readers know of noisy nocturnal intrusions that ended with the landowner inadvertently killing his own friends?

Lawyers might exclaim, "If we adopt the castle doctrine, there will be an explosion of nocturnal intrusions with an unnecessary loss of many lives." Sure, my dear lawyers, but for a very little while only. Just the time needed for thieves to learn the consequences of the new castle-law. Of course they will immediately adapt their strategy, and avoid intruding during the night. Or do you think thieves are as dumb as lawyers?

What really cries to the heavens is the contrast of communal funds invested in criminal and victim: the large majority of the expenses of the US department of Justice go the criminal, while it should be the other way around: criminals should work their whole life to pay off their infinite debt to their victim, her family and friends.

3.3 Self-Defense Laws are Written by Unworldly Bookworms

Another example of legislative ingenuousness concerns self-defense. Consider a sexual assault in Pamplona, Spain, in 2014. A woman was harassed at 8:37 in the morning of the 'Sanfermines' by a tipsy youngster who harassed her physically. After participating in the traditional bull runs her boyfriend appeared on the scene. Upon seeing his girlfriend harassed, he ran towards her and punched the assailant. The latter had to go to the hospital. The public prosecutor's claim amounted to half a year of prison and a €120,000 fine[31] for unnecessary

31 from which €60,000 were destined for the covering the assailant's hospital expenses

violence on the part of the boyfriend, and a year of prison for the assailant for sexual harassment with the *mitigating circumstance of drunkenness*.

This cries out loud for Hume's guillotine. Anything worth of calling itself a law should consider drunkenness an *aggravating circumstance*, just as it is behind the steering wheel. So I guess an ultra-stupid lawyer formulated that law. Who controls these guys? We cannot put physicists in charge of *everything* going on in society, can we?

Below follows the explicit message the public prosecutor conveys to society:

> "Come, heavy drinkers from every corner of the world, come to Pamplona! The more you drink, the less imputable you will be. If by chance you penetrate one of our beautiful girls, and a dumb local thinks he should come to her aid, our retrograde laws will have him pay all of your hospital expenses. With a bit of luck you might even meet him in prison and teach him a little lesson."

The second example of retrograde laws on self-defense comes from my own country. In 2001, an Ajax fan ran into the field during an official soccer game and threw a karate kick at the goalie, Alvarado Brown. Alvarado was barely able to avoid the kick and responded. He went "super-minimalistic", in the sense that he continued kicking the assailant after the latter had fallen to the ground. Alvarado did so instinctively, even though the whole stadium (and half the country via television) was witnessing the show. The referee took no risk, acted according to a lawyer-written booklet, and gave Alvarado a red card.[32]

The politically correct referee caused a disaster on all accounts. Alvarado's coach had to withdraw all his players from the field, thereby losing the match, in order to avoid collecting ten more red cards. The frustrated public had paid to watch soccer, but ended up seeing a poor karate exhibition: all this because of the retrograde Dutch-lawyer conception of proportionality in self-defense. Two definitions of proportional response are the following:

A "minimal response" ends when the assailant loses fighting potential.
A "super-minimal response" ends before the assailant is as badly hurt as the victim would have been in the worst case.

The first definition of proportionality is the "bookworm" kind, highly appreciated among the unworldly lawyers of

32 For non-specialists in soccer: a red card forces one to leave the field immediately. This highest punishment is meant for players who search to injure *adversary players* instead of playing the ball. The lawyers have it mixed all up, once again. Is there really no penny left in my socialist country to check the stupidest laws?

my own little country. The second one is more in line with Hume's guillotine. In Alvarado's case, the assailant threw a karate kick, which, if well executed, would have left Alvarado quadriplegic. That the victim ends up in the hospital, much less hurt than quadriplegic, is perfectly proportionate according to the second definition of proportionality. And that is the one that keeps a society alive, not the first "Christian" one.

"Such a law fosters violence, rather than discouraging it!" the Dutch bookworm lawyers shall chant in choir. Well my dear legislators: think before you speak, and think ten times before writing a law. In a regime of Hume's guillotine, an assailant will think it over twice before acting. If an assailant seeps off badly injured, he will be less of a menace to society, and a beautiful example for his hot-headed colleagues.

Here is the message the bookworm legislators issue to society:

> Whenever you feel frustrated as a fan (about every time your team loses), just run up into the field and kick whatever adversary player! With a little luck, the player responds, and gets sent off the field. You obtain three results at once: you give way to your frustration; you hurt an opponent; and you establish yourself as a hero among your half-wit comrades. Nothing will happen to you, because you are a too regular client of jail already.

Society definitely must take care of disturbed people as much as she can, but not at the price of duping innocents.

3.4 Abortion, Suicide, Pedophiles

This section discusses some practical examples of Hume's guillotine, which might help relieve some too heavily burdened Christian consciences. A third formulation of the 'is-ought' error is to consider it a moral duty to remedy other people's wrongdoings, especially with respect to life (abortion, suicide, euthanasia) and education (adoption by pedophiles, sex education at school).

If the laws of a country establish it, immoral actions are part of legal liberties, *independently of what the truth-abiding Christian thinks about it.* Of course, it is difficult to accept for a Christian, convinced of possessing moral truth, not to respond violently, but using violence stains your conscience. Non-violent responses, like yelling in the face of those wretched mothers and equally miserable butchers, that abortion is homicide, are at least unchristian and lack all elegance. If Jesus forgave and even exalted the whores, who are we to complain about boss-in-own-belly mothers? Or do we take the Pharisees' point of view? "We caught her sinning".

Whatever moral or material injustice occurs, for a Christian it is important not to forget that in the philosophical sense *only the perpetrators suffer, never the victims.* Appendix 5 explains this in more depth. This implies that an abortion only affects mother, egotistical pseudo-boy-friend (or his parents), and executive butcher, but it can impossibly affect the eternal bliss of the aborted. If God punishes failure to surviving one's zeroth birthday, what does that mean for all natural abortions? And more importantly, what does that mean for God's perfect Justice? It would be a plain theological contradiction. As far as I'm concerned, pain enough to leave my Church instantly.

We end with some mere logic. God is Almighty. He created a perfectly good world, no matter with or without spontaneous abortions. Well, the fact is that homicidal abortions do exist. Therefore, the existence of evil homicidal abortions entails a far greater good than its absence.[33] What that greater good is, I leave to those theologians that are smarter than the bookworm-legislators.

3.5 Female Discrimination

Feminism is the cruelest male invention to continue dominating women: make them believe that someday they will run 100 meters in 9.6 seconds. Truth is that the female salary is still 30% below the males', and males occupy most top positions. Hence, what is wrong with the feminist tactic?

The physical differences between men and women originate directly from our genes: even some insects and

---

33 The greater good is, in all cases of moral evil, God's love for his creature's freedom, especially for his first-born, the Devil.

fish use the XY sexual differentiation system! Given that today's medical research is not even able to eliminate the flu, it would be childish to think science could do anything against the distinction of sexes. There is no other choice but to continue living with this biological distinction. The large majority of psychological gender problems are due to abject brain-washing. Invasive treatments are always a total disaster. Instead of believing all the recent gender squabbling, the reader had better sit down and think over quietly who might be interested in promoting the "I feel like a stranger in my body" ideology. The answer is, like always, in chapter 4. Indeed, it is an excellent strategy to weaken a society: get the females to think they should be lesbian, neutral, or males, and *vice versa*. A single Muslim with a fine sabre would be able to decapitate a complete country filled with lousy pedophiles.

As anti-feministic as it may sound, the ancient biological origin of sexuality most specifically implies that a social distinction should complement the physical one. In the society of our human and ape ancestors, the female has always been more vulnerable due to her smaller size and her long pregnancy. Usually, the female took care of the social organization, while the male would occupy his time with naps (lions excel in it), fighting for leadership, or running after prey, though only in case the useless females had failed.

For mammals, the role of the mother is essential during the first years of the little one, while the educational contribution of the father joins in at a later stage. When the child is about ten years old, in Homo sapiens, both parents contribute equally, though not the same: on average the mother's love is more 'unconditional', while the father's is more 'demanding'. Exaggeration of maternal love is anti-educational pampering, that of paternal love is equals anti-educational militarism. This behavior is so universal because of the chemical program called "genes".

The best quality assessment of laws —gender laws included— requires the previously introduced economic indicator. The better the laws reflect the true nature of man and woman, the stronger the economy is able to grow (all other factors being equal). The question is not whether laws exit that lead to an improvement of both economic strength and female appreciation. The existence of laws favoring one and disfavoring the other (on sufficiently long term, of course) simply do not exist.

The author's proposal is to reward maternal education. Simple-minds like the club of Rome would object that such a law could never boost an economy, but who cares; they also predicted that we would have been out of oil around 1980 (one of their more accurate predictions). Their publications were at the basis of the decline of the heavily brainwashed WASP population in the US.[34]

34 Table 202.40 of the US National Center of Education Statistics displays childcare arrangements of 3- to 5-year-olds (children who are not yet in kindergarten). Between 1995 and 2005, the number of ethnical whites has decreased from 6.3 to 5.2; that of the blacks kept stable at 1.2; that of the Hispanics and Asians doubled from 1.3 to 2.6 thousand children. With

For an adult person to perform well economically, she must be stable psychologically. Such stability depends crucially on education, equally but not identically maternal and paternal. For this reason, in case of a separation between parents, little children tend to be allotted to the mother, unless her educational inaptitude is proven. It should not surprise that society benefits, from a purely economic point of view, from maternal reward, if well administered. What do pedophiles contribute to the national welfare? Roughly zero, because in their old age (if they reach it) they consume all their paid taxes. What do families contribute to the national welfare? Somewhere between 2 and 10 well-educated potential tax payers!

As I am not acquainted well enough with the American situation, I will mention three Dutch peculiarities. First, a growing number of feminists fear that the original cause of feminism has failed, in spite of all economic and political incentives; many Dutch women still prefer to take care of their children at home over having a job outdoors. Second, Dutch women working outside, in academic or leadership positions, are discriminated by their male peers. Such discrimination will only grow stronger and meaner, when the government persists in its politically correct yet retrograde plans to implement hard limits of female participation in high-profile positions. Third, the once-famous, now ignominious, figurehead of

---

an overall growing Catholic population, Protestants are in serious trouble. In European countries, the ex-Catholics face demographic suicide.

Dutch feminism, Heleen Mees, has been stalking and threatening her ex-lover and married former Bank of England economist Willem Buiter.[35] It is a nice example of Communist History Manipulation that Mees' name, once prominent in all Dutch newspapers, has been deleted on all feministic websites.

So back to normal behavior: what is the author's proposition for female retribution?

All mothers should earn, like civil servants directly from government, at least:

- *a salary proportional to the children's performance at school, independently of the intellectual level of the school;*
- *a pension proportional to the sum of taxes paid by all her children and family-in-law.*

For well-performing mothers, salary and pension should suffice for their being financially independent from their husbands. The salary's independence of intellectual education level helps parents making the right choice for their children. When a mother places her children in a too high-level school (normally because of personal pride), the children will not be able to keep the pace, and the mother loses salary. When she places her children in too low-level schools, the children earn less money once grown up, and the mother loses pension.

35 https://www.telegraph.co.uk/news/10691561/Top-economist-sued-by-ex-mistress-over-stalker-claims.html

Women that aspire to outdoor careers are statistically more gifted *for those careers* than average. The reason for this *a priori* is purely probabilistic. Due to the distribution of human talents, the odds decrease for an individual to excel or underperform in all fields. On the other hand, it increases for an individual to excel in a few fields, and underperform in many other fields. Albert Einstein underperformed in nearly all possible fields (apart from physics).

With a law for maternal salary and pension, more women will choose motherhood, and such a choice reduces their financial dependence on their husbands. Consequently, the market offer of female labor decreases and due to the probabilistic law of talent distribution, the average talents of competing women on the labor market rises; whence VIP women's salaries rise, due to both scarcity and higher average skills. In such a society, women find the appreciation they earn: as mothers for being irreplaceable, and outdoors, for being men's equals or even superiors in talents.

Most importantly, such a law strongly reduces the necessity for young women to find a job in nightclubs, and it certainly puts an end to that abject abuse which is poverty-driven prostitution. The only prostitutes left will be of the 'escort' type. This latter kind of prostitution will never disappear: not even in a society with perfect laws. Rather than a symbol of slavery, escort prostitution is a sad symbol of the French 18th century concept of freedom. "Liberté, égalité, fraternité", shouted the fools. They forgot to add (or simply ignored) the essential part: "for the parvenu élite". The correct interpretation of those words dates from the first century,[36] and the French Revolution was nothing but another EZ maneuver to take over power in France by tearing it up into two fratricide parties. And yes, of course the little Corsican was a free-mason. He never gave a damn about the soldiers, despite his theatrical sister-Nightingale performances. His rests presently rot away in the grandest mausoleum of France. That Mausoleum is to the French a symbol of patriotism, and to all foreigners a symbol of patriotic idiocy.

"La donna e mobile, cual piuma al vento", complains the Duke of Mantua in Verdi's *Rigoletto*. Clearly, the Duke never experienced a female hormone cycle. The more a young woman fights against her abrupt variations of hormone levels, the more self-control she obtains. When these variations reduce with time, we men will find ourselves learning strength and stability of character from women. Certainly a minority opinion, this one; though at least the male crew of Margaret Thatcher or Neelie Kroes would agree with me.

36 Yet some obscurantist Frenchman, Voltaire, wrote "écrasez l'infâme".

3.6 The Medieval US Penitentiary Regime

3.6.1. The statistics of recidivism

According to an April 2014 report of the US department of justice, Bureau of Justice Statistics,[37] 67.8% of the 404,638 state prisoners released in 2005 in 30 states faced an arrest within 3 years of release, and 76.6% within 5 years of release.

One can measure recidivism with respect to other criteria than arrest, too.

The hierarchy of strictness is the following: arrest, adjudication, conviction, incarceration, and return to prison. In this order, the recidivism percentages decrease. The above-referred paper classifies crimes in four offense classes: property crimes, violence, drug crimes, and public order offenses. Within one year after release, 36% of the property offenders return to prison, against 28% for violence, drugs, and public order. Five years after release, these figures increase to 62% and 52%, respectively. These numbers allow for a simple explanation. *For*

37 http://www.bjs.gov/content/pub/pdf/rprts05p0510.pdf

property and drug offenders, they mean that, after release, the ex-prisoners have no choice, but returning to their old bad habits. ***They are forced to by society's rules.***

In practice, they return to their old mates in the property offending business, and start all over at the bottom of that hierarchy. For violent and public order offenders, the numbers mean that the ex-prisoners do not manage to adapt to society either, although they do not necessarily return to their old trade. All these released prisoners have one thing in common, though: prison is a place that definitely reduces one's probabilities to reintegrate into the free world. The longer time one has done, the harder it is to reintegrate. Instead of being a place to help ex-convicts reintegrate into society, prison is a place that reduces such odds. As long as US prisons decrease the odds of reintegration in society, the penitentiary regime is not enlightened, but retrograde.

3.6.2 A proposal for renewal

The statistics show there is ample room for legal improvement. Hume's guillotine keeps all delinquents working in optimal conditions, for two reasons: to maintain, or find back their psychological equilibrium, and to indemnify society. Hume's guillotine requires the definition of four new classes of convicts.

First-class convicts are all those with economical potential, and willing to work long hours. They are able to work without tight supervision, and to use their own imagination and initiative. First-class convicts wear a GPS ankle bracelet and report periodically. When they have indemnified their victim(s), they are free citizens again, unless they have to do some more time. In that case, all the money they earn ends up on a private account on their name, which they are free to dispose of when released. Depending on the gravity of an offense, the court decides the number of hours per week the convict should work, and how long. Periodic unannounced visits take place to verify the convict's compliance.

Zeroth-class convicts have no economic potential. They suffer a heavy drug addiction or a severe psychiatric condition. These people reside in a hospital rather than a prison. They should work under supervision, every single one according to his or her potential. If their psychological health improves enough, the court rules whether they are set free (small crimes) or become first-class convicts (not so small crimes).

Second-class convicts have no economic potential because they never learnt a trade, yet are willing to learn one. These people populate schools rather than prisons. They follow classes and do examinations, for all kinds of trades, and all kinds of intelligence levels. Upon graduating, they promote to first-class convicts.

Third-class convicts want to work nor study, and show violent, intolerant, or asocial behavior. They live in single-store palaces *with permanently closed doors*. Nothing goes in or out except food, waste, and books on request. A team of psychologists is responsible for following the inmates' psychological state of mind. They may promote them to second-class convicts whenever they deem suitable. All contact with other people (family, friends, jailors, and psychologists) occurs over glass and phone. Each palace is equipped with elementary fitness facilities and automatic food administration mechanisms. Prisoners have the right to ask for books, and the right to ask for self-execution.

This four-class solution totally eradicates violence and recidivism, and is much cheaper for society than the present-day, forced containment-based penitentiary system.

3.7 Media Monopolization

Since Gary Allen wrote his book “the Rockefeller file” in 1976 little has changed in the monopolization of media. The Rockefellers still control all the biggest media companies. Allen had clear ideas about it:

> (..) The Rockefellers use leverage to maximize the power of their investments in industry and finance. They follow the same principle when they buy influence over education. They do not pour money into local school board races; they put their bucks into the schools that train the teachers and they finance the writing of textbooks. Now that every public school is at the mercy of the Department of Health, Education and Welfare (which Nelson Rockefeller created and ran under Eisenhower), the family couldn't care less who controls the local school board. (...) The use of psychology and propaganda, or if you will, brainwashing, is not a Communist invention. It was developed in the West in such places as the Rockefeller financed Tavistock Institute in England. While the Communists have used these tools for mind-bending, so have the Rockefellers. The hidden persuaders from Madison Avenue, the Rand Corp. think-tank or Hudson Institute, can and do manipulate public opinion. The Establishment elitists refer to it as" the engineering of consent." (...) With money the Rockefellers gained control of the media. With

> the media the family gained control over public opinion. With control over public opinion they gained control of politics. And with control of politics, they are taking control of the nation.

Of course, nothing is wrong with owning media industries, as long as there are no monopolies. They kill an economy. Things get even uglier when monopolists abuse of their power to brainwash the public. An attack like 9/11 never could have happened without the Rockefeller media monopoly, because 60% of the odds of success of such an operation depend on thoroughly misinforming the citizens from the first minute of the attack.

3.8 Rotten Example: The BBC

Even worse is BBC's performance on 9/11. After the twin tower collapses, They had their on-site reporter Jane Standley comment that a third tower, WTC7, had abruptly come down, too. What poor Jane did not know, was that at the very moment of her reporting so, WTC7 was standing upright proudly, with no sign of instability, and for all the TV public to see as a beautiful background for Jane. With this only fact, the American 9/11 report could already have saved their painstaking work to work out an idiotic conspiracy theory comprehending a few desert nomads, experts on goats.

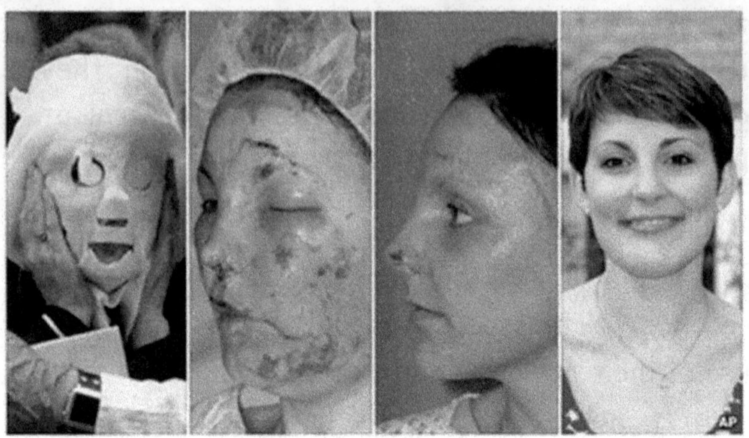

Miss Davinia Turrell (now Douglas)[38] in several stages of her recovery after the 2005 Mossad underground attack. The first photo was taken the very day 7/7 of the so-called bomb explosion. Look carefully at Davinia's hands in the first photo: they seem to be perfectly intact, and as far as her face is concerned, it is just as perfectly covered. Moreover, what seems to be her hair, it bears no burn signs at all.

Another fact might be helpful, too. Jane Standley was found murdered shortly afterwards, in a typical check-my-suicide-note pose. Dear American patriots: keep on dreaming about Bin Laden. The latter was no less a CIA patsy than Lee Harvey Oswald, by the way. Is it not significant that even the marine who officially captured Bin Laden, denies having recognized the man? CIA asset Bin Laden has been thoroughly milked until the public

38 http://nodisinfo.com/white-masked-woman-london-tube-bombings-hoax/

began to show a saturated response. Surprise, surprise: when he was not useful to the CIA any more, Bin Laden was “found”, “executed”, and “thrown into the Ocean”. The operation was so secret and urgent that the CIA apparently lacked the time to give the Americans their long-awaited proof of Bin Laden’s photograph. Oh, my dear American patriots, how many more historical facts do you need to finally convert from your paranoid blindness?

CHAPTER 4
Collective Ingenuousness

4.1 Conspiracy Characteristics

A typical ancient conspiracy is the Roman one against Julius Caesar, where a few very powerful men came together to kill another. The ingredients to a classical conspiracy are the first two ones. A "morally wrong" conspiracy needs three more ingredients:

(i)	secrecy in the preparatory phase.
(ii)	illegality of the action (killing without a legal verdict);
(iii)	mutual distrust;
(iv)	increase of personal power;
(v)	absence of honor and idealism amongst the conspirators;

A hidden conspiracy contains at least nine more characteristics:

(vi)	Secrecy during and after its execution;
(vii)	The patsy;
(viii)	invisibility of the conspirators before, during, and after the events;
(ix)	abuse of national structures (military, industrial, financial), but above all of the secret services;
(x)	careful timing of the publication of facts related to the attack;
(xi)	abundant production of contradictory testimonies at the moment and after the attack;
(xii)	a plethora of blunders during the execution;
(xiii)	abundant production of conspiracy theories after the attack and physical elimination of people with too much information;
(xiv)	pre-planned immediate destruction of all evidence

As for the ingredients (iii)-(xiv) it is possible to mention the existence of morally praiseworthy conspiracies, like that of the many German attempts to kill Hitler. The 'patsy' mentioned in ingredient (vii) is an innocent person, chosen because of an easily constructible motive or compromising personal circumstances and social connections. Ingredient (xii), the enormous blunders and botched jobs, is a direct consequence of the command structure. The group of conspirators consists of a few very powerful people. Due to the necessary invisibility of the conspirators, the latter are not able to supervise the job personally, and forced to leave the supervision to institutes that are sufficiently prone to blackmail. This does work, though understandably, multiple errors are inevitable. However, all errors can be turned into their advantage; e.g., they will confuse simple-minded investigators.

4.2 The Four Stupidest Conspiracy Theories Ever Published

Official reports are conspiracy theories like all others, the only difference being that they bear an official stamp of a governmental institute. That hardly constitutes a warranty for truth, especially if one suspects the existence of a deep or dark state. Instead of debunking all alternative conspiracy theories (which is often impossible, because they are construed by smart people paid by the very perpetrators), we here choose to debunk the stupidest ones, that is, those bearing a government stamp.

4.2.1 New York 2001

According to the official 9/11 report, nineteen Islamic fanatics seized command of four planes at exactly the same time, confusing the air traffic controllers during several essential minutes. The controllers thought it was a CIA exercise, because NORAD had planned one that very day in California. Up to here it is a curious coincidence to say the least. There are a few more issues, though:

- *Before the attack, the large majority of the US population wanted an end to Middle & Far Eastern wars. After the attack, the large majority of the US population cried out for war, endorsing additional defense expenses.*
- *The internationally admired American defense system did not get a single fighter at eyesight from the four "seized" Boeings. The latter are like turtles, in comparison to fighter jets. Although the Americans bought Russian silence for solid currency (the latter saw the tiniest details of the attack, and of course knew on forehand it would happen, like the Israeli's), American observation equipment (civil radar, military radar, and satellites) saw nothing but four plane-like objects.*
- *Bin Laden allegedly coordinated the vast operation from a Pakistani governmental prison, awaiting*

release in return for ransom. Too bad he did not even dispose of a mobile phone.

- *An alleged hijacker drives an alleged Boeing into the Twin Towers after an extremely risky pirouette that even the best American pilot is unable to reproduce. Why would Islamic terrorists take such stupid risks? Imagine the Muslim humiliation when, due to the pirouette, the Boeings failed to hit their targets...*
- *One of the alleged Boeings has all the outer features of a military drone KC767. Many witnesses saw no markings, no emblems, no logos, and no windows on the sides of drone UA175 crashed into WTC2. Specialists immediately recognized the military drone KC767 had a modified belly and carried a uranium-head missile at one of its sides.*[39] *The only goal of the depleted-uranium missile was to open a big hole for the drone to disappear completely inside the building. That allowed EZ to later claim that the drones were Boeings instead.*
- *EZ organizes a wreck of a turbine, not far from ground zero. The EZ Muppets forgot that Boeing exclusively uses Pratt & Whitney, not General Electric.*[40] *Older, now long confiscated images, reveal*

---

39 See Christopher Bollyn's trilogy on the matter. First set away contemptuously as a conspiracy theorist, now being held permanently out of publicity by EZ.

40 The CIA bunglers fulfilled criterion (xii) of the contemporary conspiracy by planting the wrong motor on Murray Street: they planted a CF(M5)6 from General Electric. Fighter Jet pilot John Lear sarcastically concludes in his interview, "The guy dropped off the wrong engine."

there was no first Boeing at all, but a missile. All historical known examples of passenger planes hitting a high-rise building show a hole in the form of half a sphere, with a diameter more or less the distance between the turbines, and 90% of the airplane debris recognizable and scattered all over the ground. The precious silhouette of the Boeing in the South Tower is obviously the result of mini-bombes placed on forehand.

- *None of the hijackers appears on surveillance camera's when entering the planes, nor walking through the airports. Apparently, they had an invisibility knob.*[41]
- *Molten steel suddenly flows out of WTC2, hours after firefighters had declared the initial fire under control. These initial fire pockets were so weak that the automatic water spraying system was sufficient to take care of them.*
- *The only surviving object was an Islamic passport. Well, there we have hard proof it was them again!*
- *A class of schoolchildren exercises the pronunciation of the words "airplane" and "steel" in presence of the president. Really funny joke, EZ, I am still fighting my hick-ups.*
- *After being discretely informed "that the nation is under attack", the President sits still, smiling like an idiot. What else can an idiot do?*

---

41 Only on sale in SF-movies.

- *The President is finally taken to some unknown safe house. The Commander-in-Chief now is EZ-puppet Dick Cheney, who presented an astonishing list of contradictory confessions as to his whereabouts on 9/11 to the 9/11 inquiry commission.*
- *In the afternoon, when the twin towers have already collapsed two hours ago, BBC's Jane Standley, standing with her back to downtown New York, reads from her papers that the 43-level WTC7 has collapsed, too, while everybody can see it standing straight up right behind her. BBC bluntly denies. Why? Because BBC knows how dumb its listeners are.*
- *Wikipedia discloses the testimony given by Norman Mineta, secretary of civil transportation (who ordered the suspension of all domestic flights), in a publicly broadcasted interrogation by the 9/11 Commission. His testimony was not included in the final 9/11 Commission Report because it represents clear proof that Vice-president Dick Cheney had all fighter jets either scrambled in the wrong directions, or forbidden to take off at all. Mineta was in the White House bunker and testifies on the moment that the alleged flight AA77 was heading for the Pentagon:*

> *"There was a young man who had come in and said to the vice president, 'The plane is 50 miles out. The plane is 30 miles out.' And when it got down to, 'The plane is 10 miles out,' the young man also said to the vice president, 'Do the orders still stand?' And the vice president*

turned and whipped his neck around and said, 'Of course the orders still stand. Have you heard anything to the contrary?' Well, at the time I didn't know what all that meant."

The real meaning of this mysterious conversation became clear to Mineta after the disaster; the vice president was referring to his own orders that all fighter jets be kept on the ground! Clearly, Dick Cheney's presence in the bunker was crucial in coordinating the 9/11 attack. His name does not sound so Islamic, by the way. Or is it a fake for Muhammad Ben Ali?

- *Convincing the civil American population of the danger of Islam was simple enough (just show them some compatriots jumping from the Twin Towers), but for the military hierarchy made up of tougher men something more was necessary: an attack on the Pentagon, the brains of America's defense system.*
- *The whole Pentagon had only one operational surveillance camera, whereas an ordinary shopping mall has thousands. The ingenuous believe that story as easily as we drink our cup of coffee.*
- *The Pentagon drone manages to disappear into a tiny 16 feet diameter hole, after having performed a physically impossible pirouette and having flown so close to earth (ramming trees and electricity poles) with a velocity that would have torn a Boeing into small pieces already at 700 meter height. Let alone*

the pirouette, which is mere EZ entertainment productions.

- *The Pentagon drone*[42] *however does not explode upon impact. Conspicuously absent are any fuel or burn marks: the surface of the penetration hole even shows an opened book with intact pages. The images that American civilians continue to upload on Youtube (and the EZ continues to remove) show the done rather convincingly.*
- *The attack onto the Pentagon had a farther-reaching goal. A day before the attack, on September 10, the secretary of defense, Donald Rumsfeld, made an astonishing declaration, reported on January 29, 2002: "According to some estimates, the destination of 2,300 billion dollars cannot be located." PBS (Public Broadcasting Services) revealed that this figure comes from the very inspector general of the Pentagon. The news that Rumsfeld gave, was not a mere explanation of a list of expenses, but a shameless declaration that the EZ-controlled military do not intend to report to society. It is clear that in ordinary circumstances Congress would have hanged Rumsfeld on the spot. What a nice coincidence! The day after 9/11 the 2,300 billion dollars were no more spoken of.*
- *During an intensive renovation of the Pentagon, all civil workers temporarily moved to Washington D.C. Only 65 of them (all employees from Resources*

---

42 https://www.youtube.com/watch?v=5cFewUG3rSY

Services) returned to the Pentagon after the renovation: mainly civil accountants, analysts, and budget managers. They had professional knowledge of the destination of the disappeared 2,300 billion dollars. The official 9/11 report declares that, "due to the impact of Flight UA77, unfortunately, 34 civil servants also died." With them, of course, also disappeared the crucial information of the origin and destination of Rumsfeld's 2,300 billion dollars.

- *The alleged Shanks Ville UA93 crash site only showed flammable mail addressed to California. Ten independent eyewitnesses firmly stated not having seen the slightest remains of an airplane crash. Not a single credible eyewitness stated having seen a plane at all. All cell phone calls, supposedly made from the alleged Shanks Ville Boeing at cruising height, were physically impossible due to the lack of coverage.*
- *Resuming, not a single Arab ever hijacked the passenger flights AA11, UA175, UA93, or UA77.*
- *Today there are not the slightest remains of the four flights UA77, AA11, UA175, and UA93. It was pure coincidence that the EZ-controlled CIA planned, that same 9/11, a secret operation of airplane-hijacking in California — obviously to assure that all the useful and competent personnel in hijacking would have been far from their posts.*
- *History Commons Alert describes the schedule of the exercises of the North American Aerospace Defense Command (NORAD). At 9:40am, on September 11,*

the "hijacking simulation" would begin, predicted as part of the NORAD exercise. Upon hearing the report of the hijacking of flight AA1, Kevin Nasypany, the NORAD commander of NEADS, Northeast Air Defense Sector, member of the team that put together the exercise, cynically deduced that "someone had started the exercises very early." Not due to incompetence!

- *The sequence of debris planting in Shanks Ville is an ode to criterion (xii) of contemporary conspiracy. The official 9/11 report declares that flight UA93, a Boeing, crashed in Shanksville, Pennsylvania, but all eye-witnesses emphatically deny both the crash and there being remains of a Boeing.*[43]
- *The public has largely forgotten that three towers came down on 9/11, not just two. The third building (WTC7), also known as the Solomon Brothers Building, collapsed, too. This giant of 47 stories contained among others the national archives of financial scandals (like the scandal revealed in 2001 of the American company, Enron). It came down in seven seconds, without any preceding damage, clearly the result of a controlled demolition. The official 9/11 report again denies what is evident. The occupants of the WTC7 building on 9/11 included the Securities and Exchange Commission, the Internal Revenue Service (IRS) Regional Council, the Department of Defense (DOD), and the Central*

43 http://911blogger.com/news/2013-02-19

Intelligence Agency (CIA). Interestingly, there was nobody in WTC7 on 9/11 long before the first impact. Forty-seven empty floors on a normal working day! How is this possible without previous warning? It is not indeed. Not only all the personnel working in WTC7 knew it would be blown, but also the New York fire fighters, and even four international broadcasting companies. Dr. Graeme MacQueen's *in-depth analysis is worth seeing, as well as all the snaky lies and misinformation of BBC trying to hide their multiple blunders with Jane Standley.*

The physico-chemical analyses of the thick (10 cm) layer of dust that covered the whole city after the 9/11 attack were published in The Open Chemical Physics Journal, 2009, 2, 7-31, by nine scientists among whom Steven Jones, in a scientific article entitled "Active Thermitic Material Discovered in the Dust from the 9/11 World Trade Center Catastrophe".

From right to left: 9/11 image of the dust-covered streets. An ordinary controlled implosion (like for WTC7) does not leave such amounts of dust. The dust is due to the instantaneous conversion of concrete into dust by explosives. In a controlled demolition the concrete remains intact, as do most of the iron grids, except that they came down on the building's

footprint. Middle: dr. Steven Jones, the highest level 9/11 physicist nobody listens to, I believe because of sheer ignorance of the large public. Third pane: micrograph of unburnt nanothermite, discovered in huge amounts in the dust. Indeed, Jones' scientific paper ascribes the collapse of the twin towers to a totally unknown explosive called nanothermite for obvious reasons.[44] *The authors were able to reconstruct the exact shape and composition of the explosive material. Years before its use, a National Laboratory Journal extensively described the military properties of nanothermite: it cuts through steel like butter, and pulverizes concrete walls like sand castles on the beach. Its advantages over classical explosives are that (i) ignition occurs at a single critical temperature, not along a trajectory; (ii) pressure changes do not set off the explosive, either, and (iii) the explosives were loaded into the twin towers as huge batteries needed to provide emergency power to all computers in case of a power failure.*

- *Just like in the Spanish attack in Madrid 2004 (Atocha), where all metal evidence (some twenty train carriages) magically disappeared (characteristic xiv of the conspiracy), in New York, too, all steel*

44 In normal thermite, used for welding iron, the two reactive components (aluminum and oxide) are on average separated by tens to hundreds of microns. In nanothermite, the two reactive components are on average separated by distances more than 10,000 times smaller. This turns a low-burning welder into an atomic bomb.

of the two twin towers was transported transnationally and molten in India. About 99% of the Spanish population still believes, to date, that Al-Qaeda or some cretin Muslim cell was responsible for the 2004 Atocha terror attack. Fact is that this very 99% of the Spanish population did not take the time to read the official conspiracy theory.

- *Although the 9/11 report does not contain the Mineta testimony, the military Journals did publish the properties of nanothermite two decades ago: selective publication is characteristic (x) of a conspiracy. This way no smart-ass investigator could claim to have found a secretly developed weapon.*
- *There are only three places in the world were the necessary amounts of nanothermite could have been produced for pulverizing the 440 meters high twin towers: Los Alamos National Laboratory, Lawrence Livermore National Laboratory, and a chemical laboratory of the Naval Surface Warfare Center – everything coordinated by Bin Laden from his miserable Pakistani coordination center (read: cattle prison).*

What can we make of all this government utter nonsense? Well, first of all, the pilots of the four passenger flights were not at all Arabs, but plain, ordinary, though highly trained, CIA pilots They simply took the planes to military bases (which explains the coverage for mobile calls) for all the passengers to be executed on the spot. During the flight, the passenger planes had "close encounters" with ordinary drones. For the non-specialist: flight controllers determine the distance of a flying object from the tower by the time elapsed between signal emission and reflected signal reception.[45] When two objects fly close, let us say, closer than 100 meter, at a distance of more than 10 km from the supervision towers, the timings do not allow for a clear distinction between the two flying objects. When moreover, two equally large flying objects cross under a very small angle, no flight supervisor is able to tell whether the two objects crossed paths, or whether they both followed a sharp-angle hyperbolic path (meaning that the object entering the close-encounter zone from below, exits downwards, too). The normal thing to assume in watch towers, is that their paths crossed. Well, one of the main 9/11 ingredients was the hyperbolic passing trick. From then on, the radar experts confounded the drone flights with those of the passengers: the supposed passenger airlines AA11, UA175, and UA77, had turned magically into simple "drones" (plane-like distance-guidable bombs). Three of the drones, targeting the twin towers and the Pentagon, had

45 The signal speed is very close to that of light in vacuum

to enter their respective buildings at such a precise location and entrance angles (these are six independent numbers for every drone, by the way) that the drones could impossibly have done the trick under distance-guidance from their launch sites.

Well, what is the obvious solution to this problem? It is a take-over of the distance-guiding from launch-site antenna's by target-site antenna's (i.e. placed inside the targeted buildings). The only necessary circumstance is some time of overlap between the two guidance systems.

That is where the drone pirouettes come into play: during the pirouette, the target-site antenna takes over command from the launch-site antenna. The moment of take-over is crucial, because it should occur on exactly that spatio-temporal window in which the drones receive both the target signal and the launch site signal. Although all of this can be done automatically, EZ took not the tiniest risk and wanted the whole operation to be commanded by eyesight, with always the back-up option of the automatic pilot.

That is where WTC7 comes into play. That building simply served as a command site. Technicians could oversee the full take-over operation from there. Of course, such a uniquely challenging project required something more than a guy behind a telescope. They might have installed three stores of hardware.

How do you get rid of all that stuff when the bombing is done? Use 30 trucks to remove all of it, under plain eye sight of the public? Evidently not. The building simply had to be demolished, together with all proof stacked inside. Preferably not with such sparkling glamor as the twin towers, but as unnoticed as possible. That is why WTC7 came down by *controlled demolition*, which is the very opposite of the microsecond conversion of concrete-into-dust demolition of the twin towers.

This is explanation is so straightforward and obvious that one cannot conclude that America collectively lost its reasoning capacity on 9/11, either by fear, or by pre- and post-brainwashing of the media.

From people inside the twin towers at the moment of impact, most deaths were among the New York firefighters, as the rest had already amply evacuated. About half an hour after the drone impact and explosion those firefighters literally spoke of "a few isolated (harmless) fire pockets", under full control. But then the towers' foundations exploded, and subsequently the stores, carefully synchronized, one by one. Trained engineers and architects immediately recognize, from merely viewing the tapes, that even thirty drone explosions do not harm the buildings in the least, and whatever concrete tower violates every possible physical law upon falling downwards, where the counterforces are the largest. And what weight was there to push the building through its concrete pillars, when all concrete had already turned into dust? Else, why was New York uniformly covered with a 10 cm thick layer of concrete-converted dust? There was no concrete on location, after the miraculous demolition, to be sure. So it was the weight of steel that weighed the floors through their concrete pillars? How funny. We had just seen that steel was flowing like huge yellowish waterfalls from the towers! Of course, at temperatures *totally out of reach* for ordinary office fires.

High time to start taking Architects and Engineers seriously, America! As long as you believe the official report, YOU are the idiot, not the truth-seeking conspiracy theorists (that is, excluding the majority: freelance writers on EZ's payroll).

4.2.2. Madrid Atocha 2004

The train explosions in Atocha were probably EZ's answer to 'wrong' (pro-Palestinian) Spanish voting behavior in the UN, or to a denial by former President Aznar to execute an EZ order (like speaking out publicly against Palestinian terror). EZ forced the Spanish secret services to execute the attack. It is quite shocking to realize that the average Spaniard has no idea of what happened on September 11, 2004. What is much worse, the average Spaniard *does not want to have an idea at all.* The timing of the attack, just before the elections, fooled them all into believing there was a political motive. All conspiracy characteristics were present, *including the spectacular evaporation of twenty train wagons, and the chemical bleaching of the thirteen remaining metal scraps.* We also have the sudden appearance, on site, of an Islamic passport. According to the Spanish official report, the conspirators are thirty Jihad Salafists and members of the radical-Islamic organization GICM, the M standing for Morocco. The officially installed research commission was headed by Paulino Rivero Baute, with Juan del Olmo acting as the judge at the Spanish National Court of Appeal („Audiencia Nacional"). Like all American judges for 9/11, Del Olmo was either bought or coerced.

If thirty Salafists and Moroccans had planned the attack, how can one explain the disappearance, in a single day, of twenty train wagons? That's a nice example of the better kind of juggling.

True, not a single Spaniard believes the official report. This means the Spanish population is not ingenuous of the personal kind. Yet, collective ingenuousness reigns in the main plains of Spain. Nobody is concerned about the role of instructing judge Del Olmo (who failed to ask the most obvious questions), nor of the police (who failed to watch a crucial backpack during 15 minutes), nor of the overnight disappearance of all exploded wagons.

Consequently, nobody considers the mere theoretical possibility that the order might have come from abroad. This does not exclude that the nearly extinct ETA, some retarded Salafists, or a castrated GICM had their little mercenary roles in the attack. However, *this whole chapter is about who gave the orders*, not about the mercenaries executing those orders in return for pay.

So what exactly determines the stubbornness of the Spanish people? Having lived there for more than five years, I can only guess the origin.

- First, most Spanish people have appreciable difficulties with reading English: the internal market is large enough to make translations and movie-doubling commercially viable.
- Second, they largely interpreted ABC's concerns about the official 9/11 report as a private fight between two Spanish media moguls.
- Third, Spain has every reason to be proud of its imperial past. It is typical of empire-based mentalities that outside their borders only backward barbarian chaos reigns.

So what Spaniard in his right mind would ever consider that the terror attack was ordered by a US mafia?

These remarks concerning the Spanish people are in no way meant disparagingly. They are nothing but a description of human nature: the larger one's (ex)empire, the higher one's fake patriotic pride. Like the British, they would not mind fighting a major war over a few rocks at the Argentinian coast. Moreover, the contrast is characteristic between how often Spaniards complain about Gibraltar (continuously), and how often the possession of Ceuta and Melilla[46] are put into question (never).

British share this mindset with Spaniards, as they lost their global hegemony in about the same historical

46 these two territories are geographically Moroccan

period. Just like the Spaniards and Americans, the British would believe an overtly idiotic governmental conspiracy theory, rather than accept the simple option that there might have existed some very badly intentioned compatriots.

4.2.3. London 2005

The Israeli Mossad was responsible for the 2005 tube bombings on July 7 in London. The Shadow Home Secretary, David Davis, declared at some point: “It is becoming more and more clear that the story presented to the public and Parliament is at odds with the facts.” Anything more explicit would have jeopardized the life of his family.

Experts believe, with reason, that nobody was really injured that day. The most notable example is the famous “white-masked woman”.[47] The BBC magazine of August 11 2010 was so stupid to show four pictures of Davinia Turrell (now known as Mrs. Douglas). On the first picture she hides her face, although both her hands are clearly visible and intact although she declared,

> "There was a loud bang and a ball of fire appeared from my left hand side and seemed to go right round me and then quickly retracted. After the explosion, the carriage was actually

---

47 http://nodisinfo.com/white-masked-woman-london-tube-bomings-hoax/

very quiet. Everyone was too shocked to scream or shout."

On the fourth picture, we see Davinia's beautiful face "after surgery". The BBC magazine forgot to mention the identity of the women in the two intermediate pictures.

Oh yes, the perpetrator's name is Mohammad Sidique Khan. Mossad counts on it that the British average IQ is high enough to recognize this as an Islamic name.

The official conspiracy theory, constructed by the commission presided by Lady Justice Carol Hallett, Judge at the English Court of Appeal, claims three Islamists from Pakistan and one from Jamaica were responsible. Well Lady Justice, you did a poor job indeed. Even high-school kids would have done a lot better. Consider the following facts:

- *Nick Kollerstrom writes in the August 2014 edition of „The Seeker", Commentary, Israel, 'Anti-Semitism', Zionism and US-UK allies that the former Israeli Mossad agent Juval Aviv had a slip-of-the-tongue: „It's easy to place a truck bomb, as we did in.... uh, as happened in London";*
- *Tony Blair and MI5 knew, admittedly, of the operation shortly in advance, because they were alerted by the Mossad;*
- *the Mossad warned Netanyahu on July 27 in his hotel in London not to leave for the TASE Conference in Liverpool Street (he was scheduled to pronounce the*

opening speech) for another 15 minutes because the attack would soon find place;

- *The half-wit or total idiot Benjamin Netanyahu publicly declared that he had been warned in his hotel at Russel Square not to leave for another 15 minutes. His declarations embarrassed both the Mossad and Scotland Yard, and left them skirmishing publicly over whodunnit;*
- *within a few hours after the explosion Galei Zahal (an Israeli military radio) announced that Scotland Yard was given a briefing shortly before the attack;*
- *Nicolas Sarkozy, not yet president of France, recognized one of the four perpetrators as an MI5 agent, having MI5 look like a bunch of imbecile amateurs. It also speaks books full of what people Sarkozy often has contact with.*

Yes indeed, my dear Mrs. Hallett, you delivered a rather poor piece of work. You must have been a perfect blackmail blank. Do you not understand that, once you speak out publicly that the Mossad threatened you, they would rather protect than kill you, in order not to confirm your very words? On the other hand, as you do not speak out publicly, you will end up like Jane Standley, “suicided” by EZ. *Faites vos jeux.* Else, your fear will send you straight into your grave.

4.2.4. Charlie Hebdo in Paris 2015

The Independent published an interview with Jack Lindblad of the Green Party of Los Angeles County Council, on January 15, 2015:

> "Speaking to PressTV, Jack Linblad claimed that the actions of the Kouachi brothers and Amedy Coulibaby, who collectively shot and killed 17 people in three separate and shocking attacks in Paris, were not acting on their extremist religious beliefs but were instead carrying out orders from the US and Mossad. Mr Linblad added that he believed the bloody attacks had been orchestrated to keep Europe under Netanyahu's thumb and to ensure the Israeli leader stays in power."[48]

For those who still doubt the French attack is an "inside job": the police found an Islamic passport on the scene, just like in Madrid and on ground zero. Seek, and ye shall find... all fourteen conspiracy ingredients.

The Paris Patsies were two French-born jihadists of Iraqi origin (that is a brilliant choice for the ingenuous public, as all ingredients are there: jihadists, Iraq, and French-born), brothers Cherif and Said Kouachi. Head of the research commission was François Moulins, chief prosecutor of Paris. His masterpiece of research

48 http://www.independent.co.uk/news/world/europe/paris-attacks-us-politician-jack-lindblad-claims-charlie-hebdo-killings-were-by-us-and-mossad-to-9979696.html

concluded that the two brothers (who died in the persecution), were the organizers. Yet the French police have not found their bodies. Oops! Did the two brothers, after having been killed, still manage to escape from the French police and secret service? That would be the first time in the history of La France! Unless... the very French Secret Service hid their bodies, as a kind deal with EZ.

Below is the cartoon that cartoonist Charbonnier had to pay for with his life. The Mossad was not amused, apparently. French President François Hollande left no doubt as to the perpetrators' identity: not Muslims, but "dark state illuminati".

Still No Terror Attacks in France*: Wait! You have time to file your wishes until the end of January...*

4.3 The Assassination of John F. Kennedy Finally Solved

4.3.1 Clint Eastwood does not mind, but there were eight shots

The typical example of a modern conspiracy is the assassination of President John F. Kennedy by the CIA on November 22, 1963 on the Dealey Plaza in Dallas, Texas. For whoever wants proof of the fact that there were eight shots, none of them fired by Oswald, it suffices to read Randolph Robertson's study, in which he synchronized the video footage by Zapruder with the acoustic tape "DictaBelt" from the motorcycle policeman, H.B. McLain. This synchronization, *made with a precision of a few milliseconds,* not only counts eight shots and their multiple echoes, but by timing the echoes it also is able to identify the three sites from where the shots originated. Four of the shots reached the president and a fifth wounded Governor Connally. The four shots triangulated the President (which means that two shots were fired from a single place), and the final shot (issued from Grassy Knoll, by the only surviving killer, James Files) exploded his skull, launching his brains all over the place, though exclusively *behind* the President.

Just before the assassination, Winston G. Lawson, CIA, ordered the motorcycle guards to retreat. No more questions asked by the 9/11 Commission, who apparently consider the order obvious. The Commission did however show keen interest in Lawson's "personal feelings" at the time: "I thought the president did not appreciate motorized policemen around". Thank you, mister prosecutor, and please keep your imbecile questions to yourself the next time.

4.3.2 Kennedy's AUW freedom speech

It is easy to imagine the CIA's frustration after their humiliation in the Bay of Pigs in Cuba (1961), followed by the missile crisis in 1962. In 1963, Kennedy signed the National Security Action Memorandum 263, which ordered withdrawing 1,000 military from Vietnam. It is very probable that Kennedy had in mind to withdraw the rest of the army from Vietnam upon re-election (in 1964). His speech in June 1963 given at the American University of Washington, was entitled "a strategy for peace". Notably, he commented that the United States were trying to approach the Soviet Union in order to begin a bilateral nuclear disarmament, and that the US would never start a war against the Soviets. Imagine the EZ panic! However, what really killed the President was not the peace speech at the American University, but his decree 11110, subject of the next section.

The mob certainly did not order the presidential killing, as any other president would have continued persecuting them. Neither did the CIA order it; certainly not Director Allan Dulles, neither Deputy Director for

Plans Richard M. Bissell Jr., nor Deputy Director Charles Cabell, who were always quite fond of Kennedy.

4.3.3. Rubinstein blackmailed by EZ

It is ridiculous to believe that Vice-president Lyndon B. Johnson ordered the assassination,[49] as his personal motivation would have been too obvious. Hence, yes, EZ ordered the assassination, and they used the heavily shaken and disoriented CIA to execute the attack.

No doubt, the mob had their part in JFK's assassination, too, but only on the mercenary level. Before directing his historical legal-conspiracy thriller, Oliver Stone tried to interview James Files, but was refused three times, "because Files did not like him". Although Stone's production lacks Files' crucial information, it contains many correct intuitions. Lee Harvey Oswald was a CIA field official. His own Agency used him as a patsy (nice firm to work for, the CIA). Possibly the mob was responsible for silencing Oswald two days later, that is, just before his first hearing. It severely blackmailed Jacob Leon Rubenstein, whose Jewish name betrays that EZ might have been close to his family. In his own words:

"Everything pertaining to what's happening has never come to the surface. The world will never know the true facts, of what occurred, my

49 his does not clear him from the strong suspicion of having cooperated, as testified by his own wife.

> motives. The people that had so much to gain and had such an ulterior motive for putting me in the position I'm in, will never let the true facts come above board to the world."

Ruby is not an ordinary hitmen: the latter are proud of their professional skills. They are mentally sick people who consider it a game to elude the police; an arrest is just a professional risk. Upon reading Ruby's quote again, one realizes there is not an ordinary hitman talking. My guess is that EZ had threatened him to kill someone he particularly cared about.

James Files (aka Sutton), a genuine hitman and responsible for exploding JFK's brains, is the only survivor, simply because he never talked. His three colleagues, James John Rosselli, who shot the president in the neck, and their bosses Charles Nicoletti and Sam Giancana, were all executed in the 1970's. Below a short fragment of Files' confession on his scouting cooperation with Lee Harvey Oswald, shortly before his boss informed him on his definitive assignment: to fire a lead-filled (exploding) bullet from the Grassy Knoll through the left eye of JFK, in case by then JFK had not received a clear head shot.

> "Lee Harvey Oswald knew that I was there but I never told him why I was there. He had just been come over and told to stay with me and to help me out and to assist in any way he could. Lee Harvey Oswald and I never discussed the

> assassination of John F. Kennedy. I discussed that with no one. Because my part of it...I had no part of the assassination at that time...all I did was go down, take the car down, take the weapons down, clean the weapons, calibrate the scopes, make sure everything was functioning properly and then know the immediate area surrounding Dealey Plaza back to the expressways and the other local highways that could be used as an extraction point to leave Dallas in case something should go wrong. At that point, I had no involvement at all in the assassination outside of that...just doing my little job that I had to do."

This is the way hitmen talk: like a computer, unaware of their own existence. Extensive details can be found in the book „Files on JFK" by Wim Dankbaar.[50] Wikipedia's page on the „CIA Kennedy assassination conspiracy theory" is in complete contradiction with Wim Dankbaar's findings; obviously, the Wikipage was ordered by EZ. Nearly all of Wikipedia's pages concerning conspiracy theories are EZ-ordered, a curious exception being the Mineta page.

Interestingly, James Files revealed that he filled his only bullet (as he was to take the last possible shot) with lead because of its explosive effect upon impact. Obviously, the Congress will never allow an independent chemical analysis of the president's remains, which are full of lead if Files is right: EZ would never let that happen.

---

50 BookSurge Publishing, December 2nd 2005

4.3.4 Kennedy's Executive Order 11,110

On June 4, 1963, President John F. Kennedy signed a decree with the authority to strip the Federal Bank of its power to print money, and to loan it to the United States Federal Government at interest. With the stroke of a pen, Kennedy declared that the privately owned Federal Reserve Bank would soon be out of business. The Christian Law Fellowship has exhaustively researched this matter through the Federal Register and Library of Congress. One may safely conclude the absence of any subsequent Executive Order repealing, amending, or superseding Executive Order 11,110. In simple terms, it is still valid. When President John Fitzgerald Kennedy signed this Order, it returned to the United States Federal Government, specifically the Treasury Department, the Constitutional power to create and issue currency without going through the privately owned Federal Reserve Bank.

4.3.5 The Federal Reserve Bank myth

A myth that all Americans live with is the charade known as the "Federal Reserve." It comes as a shock to many to discover that it is not an agency of the United States Government. The private owners (mainly the Rothschild family) designed the name "Federal Reserve Bank" to deceive, and it still does. It is not federal, nor is it owned by the government. It pays its own postage like any other corporation. Its employees are not in civil service. Its physical property is held under private deeds, and is subject to local taxation (government property is not). It is a smooth-polished engine designed to steal multi-trillion dollars from the Nation yearly. It has enabled EZ to manipulate the American economy for its own agenda and enlisted the government as its enforcer. It controls everything affecting American daily life, most importantly, its deficit.

President Kennedy's Executive Order 11,110 gave the Treasury Department the explicit authority: "to issue silver certificates against any silver bullion, silver, or standard silver dollars in the Treasury." This means that for every ounce of silver in the US Treasury's vault, the government could introduce new money into circulation based on the silver bullion physically held there. US Treasury brought more than $4 billion United States Notes into circulation in $2 and $5 denominations. $10 and $20 United States Notes never circulated but the Treasury Department was printing them the very day of Kennedy's assassination.

US Treasury issued "United States Notes" as an interest-free and debt-free currency backed by its silver reserves. The "Federal Reserve Note" issued from the private central bank of the US (the Federal Reserve Bank, also known as Federal Reserve System) looks almost like a "United States Note" from the US Treasury issued by President Kennedy's Executive Order, except one says "Federal Reserve Note" on the top while the other says "United States Note".

Most importantly, the FED started taking out of circulation all United States Notes the very day of the president's assassination. This fact alone is enough proof of EZ's order to assassinate the president. Obviously, the causality chain was the other way around; in order to eliminate all competing US Notes from the market, EZ had to sacrifice the President, for the tenth time in USA history. Federal Reserve Notes continued to serve as the legal currency of the nation. According to the United States Secret Service, 99% of all US paper "currency" circulating in 1999 are Federal Reserve Notes. Kennedy knew that if the silver-backed United States Notes were widely circulated, they would have eliminated the demand for Federal Reserve Notes. This is a very simple matter of economics. The USN was backed by silver while the FRN had none. Executive Order 11,110 should have prevented the national debt from reaching its current level (virtually all of the nearly $9 trillion in federal debt has been created since 1963) if Lyndon Johnson or any subsequent President were to enforce it. Of course LBJ did not do it himself, as he owed his new job to EZ.

4.3.6 The Warren Commission

The CIA involvement is unavoidable from the moment that President Lyndon B. Johnson appointed John J. McCloy[51] as a member of the Warren Commission. This

51 McCloy was former president of the World Bank and of the Chase Manhattan Bank, former chairman of the Council on

allegation is quite widespread (see e.g. Joan Didion's "Miami") and confirms that the Warren Commission was instituted in order to cover up EZ as the origin of the assassination. Other examples of specific expertise needed to cover up EZ: ex-CIA director and member of the Commission Allan Dulles personally supervised all hearings of CIA and FBI officials, making sure nothing compromising would issue from there.

The official 889-page report made public on September 27th 1964 concluded what any conspiracy would have done, namely, that Lee Harvey Oswald and Jack Ruby both had actuated on their own. Thank you, Warren Commission, for this magnificent piece of research. Already ripe for the garbage can before fully printed. It took the American agencies 50 years (2013) to actually do that officially. CIA-commissioned historian David Robarge wrote, with solid proof, that McCone and other CIA agents had withheld crucial information „for the good of America". Robarge's story does not tell the truth either, of course. It simply abuses of the fact that McCone, who died in 1991, cannot defend himself anymore. Everything goes, as long as it helps erasing EZ trails.

In 1976 the Congress established the House Select Committee on Assassinations (HSCA) for rehabilitating the heavily damaged Warren Commission. HSCA declared the validity of Kantor's testimony, which the

---

Foreign Relations, former trustee of the Rockefeller foundation, former chairman of the Ford Foundation, yet all but a homicide investigator.

Warren Commission had previously confuted. Their 1979 Final Report reads:

> Ruby's shooting of Oswald was not a spontaneous act, in that it involved at least some premeditation. Similarly, the committee believed it was less likely that Ruby entered the police basement without assistance, even though the assistance may have been provided with no knowledge of Ruby's intentions... The committee was troubled by the apparently unlocked doors along the stairway route and the removal of security guards from the area of the garage nearest the stairway shortly before the shooting... There is also evidence that the Dallas Police Department withheld relevant information from the Warren Commission concerning Ruby's entry to the scene of the Oswald transfer.

These sentences all shout out "conspiracy", without mentioning the word itself. But there we are: the committee is "troubled". I am quite troubled, too: by the committee's absolute lack of courage to stand up for the truth.

4.3.7 Gerald Ford's perjury in written

Gerald R. Ford changed ever so slightly the Warren Commission's main sentence on the place where a bullet entered President John F. Kennedy's body. Mr. Ford's change strengthened the Warren conclusion that a single bullet entered through Kennedy's neck, exited through his throat, again entered and exited Gov. John B. Connally's body, in order to finally bounce off the car and explode the president's brains — a crucial element in the Warren deduction that Lee Harvey Oswald was the sole gunman. Mr. Ford, who was a member of the commission, wanted a change to show that the bullet entered Kennedy "at the back of his neck" rather than in his uppermost back, as the commission originally wrote. After Dankbaar had demonstrated the Warren report was but a pile of lies, *Mr. Ford was so kind to stipulate, "I intended the change in order to clarify meaning, not to alter history"*. I literally fell off my chair from a burst of laughter upon reading Ford's silly comment. Poor America — if this characterizes the moral integrity of your presidents you are one hundred yards below sea level.

4.4 USS Liberty: High Treason of the National Congress

4.4.1 Lieutenant on the bridge of the USS Liberty speaks out

James Ennes retired from the Navy in 1978 as a lieutenant commander after 27 years of enlisted and commissioned service. He was a lieutenant on the bridge of the USS Liberty on the day of the attack. His book on the subject,

Assault on the Liberty (Random House, 1980), is a "Notable Naval Book" selection of the US Naval Institute and was "editors' choice" when reviewed in The Washington Post. The following text is taken from the article „Assault On The Liberty: The True Story Of The Israel Attack On An American Intelligence Ship" by James Ennes, survivor of the attack.

> Twenty-six years have passed since that clear day on June 8, 1967 when Israel attacked the USS Liberty with aircraft and torpedo boats, killing 34 young men and wounding 171. The attack in international waters followed over nine hours of close surveillance. Israeli pilots circled the ship at low level 13 times on eight different occasions before attacking. Radio operators in Spain, Lebanon, Germany and aboard the ship itself all heard the pilots reporting to their headquarters that this was an American ship. They attacked anyway. And when the ship failed to sink, the Israeli government concocted an elaborate story to cover the crime. There is no question that this attack on a US Navy ship was deliberate. This was a coordinated effort involving air, sea, headquarters and commando forces attacking over a long period. It was not the "few rounds of misdirected fire" that Israel would have the world believe. Worse, the Israeli excuse is a gross and detailed fabrication that disagrees entirely with the eyewitness recollections of survivors. Key American leaders

call the attack deliberate. More important, eyewitness participants from the Israeli side have told survivors that they knew they were attacking an American ship.

4.4.2 Israeli pilot disobeyed orders

Fifteen years after the attack, an Israeli pilot approached Liberty survivors and then held extensive interviews with former Congressman Paul N. (Pete) McCloskey about his role. According to this senior Israeli lead pilot, he recognized the Liberty as American immediately, so informed his headquarters, and was told to ignore the American flag and continue his attack. He refused to do so and returned to base, where he was arrested. Later, a dual-citizen Israeli major told survivors that he was in an Israeli war room where he heard that pilot's radio report. The attacking pilots and everyone in the Israeli war room knew that they were attacking an American ship, the major said. He recanted the statement only after he received threatening phone calls from Israel. The pilot's protests also were heard by radio monitors in the U.S. Embassy in Lebanon. Then-U.S. Ambassador to Lebanon Dwight Porter has confirmed this. Porter told his story to syndicated columnists Rowland Evans and Robert Novak and offered to submit to further questioning by authorities. Unfortunately, no one

> in the U.S. government has any interest in hearing these first-person accounts of Israeli treachery. Key members of the Lyndon Johnson administration have long agreed that this attack was no accident. Perhaps most outspoken is former Chairman of the Joint Chiefs of Staff Admiral Thomas Moorer. "I can never accept the claim that this was a mistaken attack," he insists. Former Secretary of State Dean Rusk is equally outspoken, calling the attack deliberate in press and radio interviews. Similarly strong language comes from top leaders of the Central Intelligence Agency, National Security Agency (some of whose personnel were among the victims), National Security Council, and from presidential advisers such as Clark Clifford, Joseph Califano and Lucius Battle. A top-secret analysis of Israel's excuse conducted by the Department of State found Israel's story to be untrue. Yet Israel and its defenders continue to stand by their claim that the attack was a "tragic accident" in which Israel mistook the most modern electronic surveillance vessel in the world for a rusted-out 40-year-old Egyptian horse transport. Despite the evidence, no US administration has ever found the courage to defy the Israeli lobby by publicly demanding a proper accounting from Israel.

It is difficult to imagine a more explicit testimony. All the proofs are here!

4.4.3. The cowardly reaction of Congress is high treason

> Most members of Congress respond to inquiries about the Liberty with seemingly sympathetic promises to "investigate." Weeks or months later they write again to report their "findings": "The Navy investigated in 1967 and found no evidence that the attack was deliberate," they say." Israel apologized, calling the attack a tragic case of misidentification, and paid damages for loss of life, injuries and property damage. The matter is closed. The fact is, however, that the Navy's "investigation" examined only the quality of the crew's training, the adequacy of communications and the performance of the crew under fire. The Navy was forbidden to examine Israeli culpability and Navy investigators refused to allow testimony showing that the attack was deliberate or that Israel's excuse was untrue.

In my view the full Congress committed high treason. Nothing stands in the way for the Nation to prosecute the Congress members that are still alive today. If the Nation's prosecution refuses to do so, they are liable of high treason, too.

4.4.4. The Navy blocked all testimony about Israeli actions

Instead of determining whether the attack was deliberate, the Navy blocked all testimony about Israeli actions. No survivor was permitted to describe the close in machine-gun fire that continued for 40 minutes after Israel claims all firing stopped. No survivor was allowed to talk about the life rafts the Israeli torpedo men machine-gunned in the water. No survivor was permitted to challenge defects and fabrications in Israel's story. Even my eyewitness testimony as officer-of-the deck was withheld from the official record. No evidence of Israeli culpability was "found" because no such testimony was allowed. To survivors, this was clearly not an investigation. It was a cover-up. (...) Unfortunately, the playing field often seems uneven. The cover-up side heavily outnumbers its critics, and is allowed tactics rarely tolerated from others. Criticism of Israeli policies is seen as "attacks on the Jewish homeland." Pro-Israel debaters charge that Israel's critics are "disciples of hate," and "pathological haters of Israel and all things Jewish."[52] (...) Despite a near

52 The language gets worse. Prodigy allows Israel's critics to be called "sodomists," and "derriere bussing anti-Semites." The Washington Report on Middle East Affairs, which prints an update on progress toward a congressional investigation every year on the June anniversary of the tragedy, comes in for special vitriol. The magazine is described almost daily as I a

media blackout, and such invectives directed at publications that defy it, Americans do continue to support the USS Liberty and its survivors' association.

Dear Lieutenant Ennes Jr.: your „media black-out" is nothing but „EZ media monopolization", as described in chapter 3.7 of this book. Here we finally meet our first honest man, who has the courage to stand up for truth, but alas... he happens to be as ingenuous as a dove in a cage.

4.5 Cleland, Cheney, Jones, Powell

4.5.1 Senator Cleland's expulsion from the 9/11 commission

David Kubiak posted an accurate overview[53] of Senator Cleland's expulsion from the 9/11 commission. Max Cleland was one of the few commissioners untainted by conflicts of interest and certainly the most outspoken with regard to the facts. By June 2003 Cleland was railing loudly against the Administration for "slow-walking" cooperation, their insistence on "minders", and the "political coordinator" in Ashcroft's Justice Department

---

hate rag." Yet Prodigy's censors often reject even mild and factual rebuttals of such charges as "insulting."

53 //911research.wtc7.net/cache/post911/commission/daschel_pnac_commission.html

who was to check all the Commission's information. Many disappointed victim family groups stated privately that Cleland was the only commissioner they would trust.

> Then on July 11, Tom Daschle suddenly and inexplicably nominated Cleland for one of the Democrat controlled board seats in the Export-Import Bank. The nomination required a presidential OK, but if approved would expel Cleland from the 9/11 Commission since no commissioner could simultaneously hold a federal post. So Daschle had knowingly put the fate of the Administration's harshest 9/11 critic into the hands of the Bush team itself. Cleland for his part refused to shut up, "As each day goes by we learn that this government knew a whole lot more about these terrorists before September 11th than it has ever admitted." (NY Times 10/26/03) He was also the only member to speak out against the Commission leaders' deal allowing the White House to severely limit and censure access to requested Bush briefing documents. As Cleland raged to Wolf Blitzer on CNN (11/13/03), "This is a scam, it's disgusting. America is being cheated... We shouldn't be making deals. If somebody wants to deal, we issue subpoenas. That's the deal." That may have been Cleland's idea of the deal, but it was also apparently the last straw. Nine days later Bush confirmed Cleland's Ex-Im Bank appointment and purged him from the Commission for good. The ball then returned Daschle's court

> as he alone had the authority to appoint Cleland's successor. The Family Steering Committee, which monitors the Commission's proceedings on behalf of many victim family groups, lobbied hard for another commissioner they could believe in — someone who would be as fearless, focused and candid as Cleland, and help allay their increasing qualms. (...) Daschle could not be pushed around by just anyone however. He fearlessly defied all victim group requests and New York editorials recommending a family member for the post, as well as thousands of faxes and emails begging him to choose Kristen above all. Daschle not only spurned these appeals, he flabbergasted everyone by appointing New School University's controversial president, Bob Kerrey, to the post. (...) PNAC has been the clearest voice promoting US control of the oil rich Middle East states; the loudest boosting military spending, full spectrum dominance, and space war tech; and the most wistful (in 2000) publicly lamenting that all its grand designs would take forever to realize without *"some catastrophic and catalyzing event — like a new Pearl Harbor."*

Upon leaving the Commission former Senator Cleland said his famous words:

> "If this decision stands, I, as a member of the commission, cannot look any American in the eye, especially family members of victims, and say the

> commission had full access. This investigation is now compromised."

The Washington Post reports the White House has agreed to allow four members of the 10-person committee have varying degrees of access to the classified presidential briefings. Furthermore, the White House places restrictions on what briefings are shareable with the rest of the commission, and it claims the right of review of all notes that commissioners take concerning the documents. This is all pure and hard evidence that President Lyndon Johnson orchestrated the bluntest cover-up of all times: a slap in the face of every sane American.

4.5.2 Dick Cheney: EZ Puppet

It was impossible NOT to contradict Dick Cheney's declarations, because the latter had been contradicting himself repeatedly. The real meaning of this mysterious conversation between Cheney and the officer became clear to Mineta after the disaster; the vice president was referring to *his own orders* that all fighter jets be kept on the ground! That is the reason why Cheney tried every possible lie to weaken Mineta's granite testimony. It proves much too clearly[54] that Dick Cheney, highest in command for being Vice-President in the absence of the

54 Actually Mineta did not speak out his mind explicitly on this point – which is the reason why he is still alive today

President himself, ordered all fighter jets either to be scrambled in the wrong direction or to stay put. Wikipedia mentions none of this: the page on Dick Cheney is a sad farce. Any sane court would condemn him to immediate execution for high treason, murder of thousands of American innocent civilians, and direct help to a criminal organization.

4.5.3 Steven Jones discovers nanothermite in New York dust

Nine scientists (among whom Steven Jones) published the physico-chemical analyses of the thick (10 cm) layer of dust that covered the whole city of New York after the 9/11 attack in *The Open Chemical Physics Journal*, 2009, **2**, 7-31. They entitled their article "Active Thermitic Material Discovered in the Dust from the 9/11 World Trade Center Catastrophe". It shows that the dust was a mixture of the concrete walls of the WTC buildings and of huge amounts of partly bunt explosives. The reader probably knows that concrete, when thrown of a very high building, never transforms into dust. This phenomenon is independent of the height of the building, because the friction with the air causes the falling velocity to saturate. The saturation velocity depends a little bit on the shape of the falling object. The only way to transform concrete into dust is the large-scale use of explosives. In the collapse of the twin towers, the explosive was largely unknown and never used before: "nanothermite." Jones and colleagues were able to reconstruct the exact shape and composition of the explosive material.

Years before its use, an American National Laboratory Journal extensively described the chemical properties and military applications of nanothermite. They proved that nanothermite cuts through steel like butter, or pulverizes concrete walls like sand castles on the beach. Its advantages over classical explosives are that

---

- *ignition occurs at a single critical temperature, and not along a trajectory (as is the case for ordinary thermite, used for welding steel rails, for example);*
- *sudden pressure changes do not set off the explosive;*
- *neither do sudden temperature changes, moisture changes, nor magnetic changes.*

Just like in the Spanish attack in Madrid (2004), the way all evidence was destroyed, reveals a deliberate, carefully prepared plan. For New York it meant to get rid of all steel and have it molten abroad. Therefore, ground zero became a huge traffic pit, while the police threatened curious photographers with confiscating their camera, "for the sake of national security and the orderly execution of expert investigation of the evidence on ground zero".

Jones' research is, on its own, already foolproof. Both towers were replete with tons of nanothermite. The pity is that the average public does not have the specific scientific/engineering background to judge the conclusiveness of his analysis.

4.5.4 Secretary of State Colin Powell

As was the case in the days leading up to the Persian Gulf War, Powell was initially opposed to sending the army into Iraq, and in favor of a policy of containment. Man of honor, he had always criticized the US support for the 1973 coup in Chili. In an interview, Powell had said:[55]

> "With respect to your earlier comment about Chile in the 1970s and what happened with Mr. Allende, it is not a part of American history that we're proud of."

Powell had no idea to what extent the Bush administration, who wanted Saddam removed by force, abused of him. He had often clashed with Cheney and Rumsfeld, who were planning an Iraq invasion even before the September 11 attacks.[56] The main concession Powell wanted before he would offer his full support for the Iraq War was the involvement of the international community in the invasion, as opposed to a unilateral approach. That was exactly where EZ wanted him: let Powell take the blame, and let us do the fighting!

Powell later recounted how Vice President Dick Cheney made fun of him before he gave the UN speech. In September 2005, Barbara Walters asked Powell about the speech, to which Powell responded that it was a "blot" on

55 See the site https://fas.org/irp/news/2003/02/dos022003.html

56 See the testimony by Richard Clarke in front of the 9/11 Commission

his record. He went on to say, “It will always be a part of my record. It was painful. It's painful now.”

At times, infighting among the Powell-led State Department, the Rumsfeld-led Defense Department, and Cheney's office had the effect of polarizing the administration on crucial issues, such as what actions to take regarding Iran and North Korea; Powell was always the peaceful party.

On September 13, 2004, Powell testified before the Senate Governmental Affairs Committee, acknowledging that the sources who provided much of the information in his February 2003 UN presentation were “wrong” and that it was “unlikely” that any stockpiles of WMDs would be found. Powell surely was ingenuous, but he was no coward.

4.6 The EZ Assignment of Prime Minister Tony Blair

4.6.1 Invasion of Iraq

Simon Tisdall writes the following in The Guardian on October 18th 2015:

> The officials [whose identity has been kept secret by The Guardian, note of JS] said part of the Blair-Bush understanding at Crawford,

followed up at a subsequent meeting at Camp David, Maryland, in September 2002, was that evidence that Iraq presented an urgent threat through its alleged attempts to obtain weapons of mass destruction would be published in London. This was the genesis of that month's Downing Street "dodgy dossier", supposedly summarising intelligence assessments. Prepared by No 10's communications chief, Alastair Campbell, the dossier laid exaggerated stress on the threat posed to Britain by Saddam's missiles and alleged WMD. In agreeing to do this, a senior military intelligence officer has told the Chilcot inquiry, Blair in effect became chief propagandist for Bush's Iraq invasion project in Britain and the US. The Guardian account in July 2002 makes clear that despite his insistence on giving Saddam a chance to comply with resumed UN resolutions on weapons inspections, Blair did not expect this to happen. When Saddam unexpectedly did comply, and when UN inspections under Hans Blix found no WMD, Blair and Bush disregarded their findings and opposed their continuation. (...) The officials told the Guardian that Bush and Blair had already agreed in Crawford the previous April that, knowing they would be likely to face insuperable security council opposition, both would adopt the position that invasion and regime change targeting Saddam were allowable under existing UN resolutions. This is exactly what happened.

Four years earlier the basic roles were already agreed upon, as testified in written by Richard Norton-Taylor (The Guardian, May 12, 2011):

> A top military intelligence official has said the discredited dossier on Iraq's weapons programme was drawn up "to make the case for war", flatly contradicting persistent claims to the contrary by the Blair government, and in particular by Alastair Campbell, the former prime minister's chief spin doctor. (...) The document is one of a number released by the Chilcot inquiry. They include top secret MI6 reports warning of the damage to British interests and the likelihood of terrorist attacks in the UK if it joined the US-led invasion of Iraq. However, a newly declassified document reveals that Sir Kevin Tebbit, then a top official at the Ministry of Defence, warned the defence secretary, Geoff Hoon, in January 2003 that the US would "feel betrayed by their partner of choice" if Britain did not go along with the invasion. Despite its concerns, MI6 told ministers before the invasion that toppling Saddam Hussein "remains a prize because it could give new security to oil supplies". Laurie's memo raises questions about the role of Sir John Scarlett, chairman of the Joint Intelligence Committee, who later became head of MI6."

One thing is clear, however: Chilcot's findings shall never see the light, and Blair will go free. Not because Blair is so powerful; his employer is.

4.6.2 Office of the Quartet Representative

After fulfilling his term as British prime minister in 2007, which he abused to push the destruction of the Middle East, Tony Blair[57] judged it his moral duty to partake in the Middle East peace envoy as the „Office of the Quartet Representative".[58] Peter Oborne writes about Blair's opportunism in the Telegraph, September 23, 2011:

> Much remains mysterious about Mr Blair's repeated visits to Tripoli over the past few years. But they display the essential characteristic of the jet-setting billionaire lifestyle he has enjoyed ever since leaving Downing Street in June 2007: an extraordinary confusion of public duty and private interest. (...) Few Kuwaitis are prepared to speak out publicly, because it is illegal to criticise the Emir. But Nasser Al Abolly, a leading Kuwaiti pro-democracy campaigner, said he had heard from good sources that Mr Blair had

57 See the bibliography in the site "http://ingenuousness.org/a2007".

58 This is an international Forum constituted by the EU, the US, Russia and the United Nations, aimed at forging peace in the Middle East.

> been paid 12 million dinars, about £27 million. "I believe this amount is exorbitant," Abolly told us.

The rest of the article shows that Tony Blair is actually behaving as if he were on a mission from the JP Morgan bank.

4.7 What Godfrey Bloom Said; What He Pretended

Godfrey Bloom was a member of the European Parliament (MEP) for the United Kingdom Independence Party (UKIP). Possibly he was also an office boy of EZ paving the way for a European Privatized Federal Bank "à la Américaine", scilicet, owned and controlled by EZ. In that case Bloom's task would be to discredit the European Banks and the European banking system, accusing it of corruption and immorality. When enough ingenuous Europeans would swallow Bloom's crap, and the European banking system collapsed, the American Fed would kindly come to our rescue.

In 2013, May 21, UKIP-MEP Godfrey Bloom kindly tells the European Parliament's President and Commissioner in Strasbourg what he's been telling them for years.

Whence, either the President and Commissioner are getting dumb, or they do hear him, but Bloom is a single-tune music box. Here is the full transcript of his tirade:

"Mr. President, I rise again, I am afraid, to make the same old hoary speech that I have been making here for several years. That is: it is my opinion that you do not really understand the concept of banking. All the banks are broke. Bank Santander, Deutsche Bank, Royal Bank of Scotland: they are all broke. And why are they broke? It is not an act of God; it is not some sort of tsunami. They are broke because we have a system called fractional reserve banking, which means that banks can lend money that they do not actually have. It is a criminal scandal and it has been going on for too long. To add to that problem you have moral hazard — a very significant moral hazard — from the political sphere, and most of the problems start in politics and Central Banks, which are part of the same political system. We have counterfeiting, sometimes called Quantitative Easing, but counterfeiting by any other name: the artificial printing of money for which, if any ordinary person did, they would go to prison for a very long time. Yet governments and Central Banks do it all the time. Central Banks repress the amount of interest rates so we do not have the real cost of money, and yet we blame the retail banks for manipulating the LIBOR. The sheer effrontery of this is quite astonishing. It is Central Banks, yes, Central Banks, that manipulate interest rates, Commissioner. Plus, underneath all this, we talk loosely — in a rather cavalier fashion, do we not — about deposit

> guarantees. So when banks go broke through their own incompetence and chicanery, the taxpayer picks up the tab! It is theft from the taxpayer! Until we start sending bankers — and I include central bankers and politicians — to prison for this outrage, it will continue".

His formidable speech betrays the EZ technique: first convince the most ingenuous MEPs (British included) that the European banking system is corrupt, bankrupt, and morally reprehensible. When enough MEPs support him, EZ has some well-known banker with excellent reputation warn the European Parliament that without a Federal Bank Europe will go bankrupt. Once the EuroFed is established, and eaten up graciously by the American Federal Bank, EZ will be in full control of both Europe and the US. EZ already controls Israel, Egypt, Turkey, and Saudi Arabia. That is the very reason that Medvedev is talking nuclear war: the Russians know that this is their last opportunity to use their rusting nukes.

4.8 CIA Officer Nuland Plays Dirty With Kiev's Neo-Nazi's

In 2013 the CIA tried to force a coup, with the brown shirts of Kiev, that would oust the democratically elected president of Ukraine. Luckily for Ukraine and for the rest of the world, the CIA coup failed. Implicated people are Victoria Nuland, John McCain and Chris Murphy, all three somehow connected with EZ. The continuous CIA activity in Kiev aims at toppling the Ukrainian government. Once it falls in the hands of EZ, Russia will be in enormous military trouble. Robert Parry writes July 13, 2015, an article in Consortium News, entitled "The Mess that Nuland Made":

> Assistant Secretary of State for European Affairs "Toria" Nuland was the "mastermind" behind the Feb. 22, 2014 "regime change" in Ukraine, plotting the overthrow of the democratically elected government of President Viktor Yanukovych while convincing the ever-gullible U.S. mainstream media that the coup wasn't really a coup but a victory for "democracy." To sell this latest neocon-driven "regime change" to the American people, the ugliness of the coup-makers had to be systematically airbrushed, particularly the key role of neo-Nazis and other ultra-nationalists from the Right Sektor. For the U.S.-organized propaganda campaign to work, the coup-makers had to wear white hats, not brown shirts.

The article also mentions the presence of Islamic fighters in Ukraine. Of course, there is nothing strange about Islamists joining the Ukrainian brown shirts, once you know that both Toria and ISIS get their orders from EZ. On January 2nd, 2015, RT News published the following interesting article about filmmaker Oliver Stone:

> The armed coup in Kiev is painfully similar to CIA operations to oust unwanted foreign leaders in Iran, Chile and Venezuela, said US filmmaker Oliver Stone after interviewing Ukraine's ousted president for a documentary. Stone spent four hours in Moscow talking to Viktor Yanukovych, who was deposed from power during the February 2014 coup, the filmmaker wrote on his Facebook page. (...) The filmmaker added that the events in Kiev, which led to collapse of the Ukrainian government and imposition of a new one hostile towards Russia, were similar to those in other countries, which he called "America's soft power technique called 'Regime Change 101'." Historically those were CIA-perpetrated coups against Iranian Prime Minister Mohammad Mosaddegh in 1953 and Chilean President Salvador in 1973 - both leaders with policies undesired by Washington's boss, the EZ mafia. More recently there was the 2002 coup in Venezuela, where President Hugo Chavez was briefly deposed "after pro and anti-Chavez demonstrators were fired upon by mysterious shooters in office buildings" and the anti-government protests against Chavez's successor Nicolas Maduro, which "was almost toppled by violence aimed at anti-Maduro protestors," as Stone put it.

Stone's critical assessment of the Ukrainian crisis provoked a storm of comments from pro-Ukrainian Facebook users, who accused Stone of taking embezzled money from Yanukovych, spreading Kremlin propaganda, and so forth.

4.9 The Next EZ Farce: 28 Pages of Fiction

In April 2016 Saudi Arabia threatens to pull $750 billion in U.S. assets if the Congress passes a bill making the Saudi's liable for 9/11-related lawsuits, while Obama "is thinking hard" on declassifying 28 pages EZ-forged crap documents which allegedly prove the Saudi's involvement in the 9/11 disaster. If the tension were real, it would mean that EZ was losing control over the Saudi's, their age-old war partner, which would of course be excellent news. However, the tension is a fake. Consequently, the families of the victims will be going through hard times again, over what they think are truth-revealing secret documents. On a global scale, the consequence of publishing fake "classified documents" is that nobody will believe the truth anymore when it finally appears in print, with all explicit proofs of EZ's principal role.
So what is the essence of EZ's strategy? As written in the Mossad's Emblem, deception and the art of false appearances.

Does EZ plan a war against Syria? First, respect a six-month brainwashing time for Washington Post and New York Times to fulminate against Iraq's use of chemical weapons. Second, in the meantime accumulate as much Sarin as you possibly can in Israel, thanks, among others, to the mentally stripped Dutch fools who do not care what El Al transports via Amsterdam Airport. Third, buy some stickers with the Arab text “made in Iran”, or Syria, and have them fixed on top of the Sarin containers. New York Times and Washington Post will do the rest: three weeks of brainwashing and every American is convinced that Syria and Iran used Sarin to kill civilians.

Of course, EZ wants to occupy Syria. They want to be the directing board deciding over the question whether the Iran-Syria pipelines are going to be implanted in Syria, or the Yemen-Turkey pipelines, or both. Sorry to tell you: despite all appearances, EZ already won the war, and Israeli militaries control the country.

4.10 President Roosevelt’s Repeated High Treasons

Below follows a quote from the article “Declassified memo: President Franklin D. Roosevelt knew of imminent Japanese attack”, published by Jacqui Goddard, December 4, 2011, in The Telegraph:

> On the 70th anniversary of Pearl Harbour, the attack that propelled America into the Second World War, a declassified memo shows that Japanese surprise attack was expected. (...) The memo, now held at the Franklin D. Roosevelt Presidential Library and Museum in upstate New

> York, has sat unpublicised since its declassification 26 years ago. Its contents are revealed by historian Craig Shirley in his new book "December 1941: 31 Days that Changed America and Saved the World." Three days after the warning was delivered to the White House, hundreds of Japanese aircraft operating from six aircraft carriers unleashed a surprise strike on the US Navy's base at Pearl Harbour, wiping out American battleships, destroyers and air installations. A total of 2,459 US personnel were killed and 1,282 injured. (...)

It is funny that Jacqui Goddard warns America to learn from Pearl Harbor, at the end of his article. Jacqui writes in this same paper (not quoted above) that there was no conspiracy. So Jacqui, please tell me, which of the fourteen ingredients of the modern hidden conspiracy are missing? Just remember the orders to station the fighter jets in a star-like formation, with the helices toward the center: this is solid proof that someone high in the hierarchy wanted to maximize the casualties.

Goddard is a precious example of collective ingenuousness: he correctly senses that "conspiracy theorist" is a synonym for lunatic, and dedicates a whole paragraph against them. Yet he fails to recognize the obvious conspiracy character of the official 9/11 report. Goddard's ingenuousness is of the "collective" kind, and not of the professional kind, because he always chooses the safe side, the politically correct side. That choice is common to everybody, not typical of journalists.

Appendices

Root of Ingenuousness: Misunderstanding the Human Spirit

Available on the site
www.matchliterary.com/patriotic-ingenuousness

Appendix 1: Non-Human Spirit

Appendix 2: Human Spirit

Appendix 3: QM and Spirit

Appendix 4: Causality and Spirit

Appendix 5: Laws of Human Spirit

EPILOGUE
Does this book come late?

Ay, at least ten years.

The United States of America are not the country of unlimited opportunities anymore. For the first time in history, Mexican return in 2016 surpassed emigration. Please help me out explaining these well- known facts:

- *Americans have the most advanced technology in the world in a lot of industrial sectors;*
- *Americans work significantly more hours per year than do Europeans, mainly due to the exceptionally few holidays per year;*
- *Americans have a relatively slender bureaucracy, and therefore waste much less on incompetent bureaucrats than Europeans; in my own country (Netherlands) the government officials were so incompetent they did not even manage to get an Italian-made fast train running on specifically built track.*
- *Americans have a modest social security system and many cases of severe poverty.*

In one sentence: Americans produce better with less expense, yet their average wealth is much lower than in Europe. In my view, this is possible only if the US are being sucked to death by a huge parasite.

The US parasite consumes trillions of dollars yearly on wars with essentially no returns, except coffins.

The US parasite consumes trillions of dollars on interest due to huge to loans graciously offered by the Federal Bank.

The US parasite consumes trillions of dollars because they spend nearly all the collected taxes on secret military operations.

History shows that too much wealth softens the moral strength of a culture to such an extent that it collapses altogether: the old Egyptians, the old Greeks, the old Romans, they all went straight to ruin due to a morally depraved ruling class. Yet the American supremacy stands already undisputed since the Second World War, with a population that is on average more virtuous than the European one. The only reason is that the Americans are poor on average.

Meanwhile the wars go on. Using your people, your money, your equipment, EZ conquered Afghanistan and Iraq, managing to turn it into an awful mess. Who harvests the blame? NATO and the US, who would not have wanted those wars in the first place, had Mr. Rockefeller not brainwashed you into believing a Weapons-of-Mass-Destruction story. Instead of getting excited for the vote of a puppet president,[59] why do you not demand referenda (popular votes) on starting foreign wars?

Any president who remotely thinks of executing Decree 11,110 is a dead president. Any CIA head who dares to oppose EZ's directives is a dead CIA head. Any army official who dares oppose EZ's directives is a dead army official.

Who does not remember Colin Powell's face in the UN when he had to declare all that nonsense on Iraq's weapons? His mouth was saying yes, his face and eyes were shouting no.

Everything started with the Israeli army deliberately destroying the USS Liberty on June 1967. According to James Ennes, the naval inquiry was a shameful cover-up. In an interview with the Washington Post Admiral Moorer stated:

> "To suggest that they [the Israeli's] couldn't identify the ship is ... ridiculous. Anybody who could not identify the USS Liberty could not tell the difference between the White House and the Washington Monument."

There was no diplomatic crisis, hardly any compensation for victims' families, but instead a shameless cover-up. Of

59 Remember Obama's lofty ideals before entering the oval office: he did not succumb to EZ's military requirements, but warmly embraced them. Sorry for you, Obama, but you will never make it to the heart of EZ, because of your non-Jewish origin, no matter how much you circumcise yourself.

course the Israeli army bears no responsibility. These poor guys only did what EZ commanded them to do.[60] At that time, EZ felt strong enough to give it a try; they had enough American Congressmen in their pocket, and controlled enough of the Navy hierarchy. Obviously, the choice was not an easy one. That is why it took the Israeli's so long to attack the USS Liberty: EZ was conferring whether the time was ripe. Kennedy's assassination and the 9/11 experience only made them bolder. Given the collective American ingenuousness they now feel, and are, all-powerful.

It is a sad truth for us Europeans that EZ controls our own secret services, too. Who profits from all the Syrian refugees, from the European bombings? Not Christians, nor Muslims, nor Americans, nor Jews, *but only EZ.* When Christians, Jews, or Muslims fight among each other, *EZ celebrates.* As the Romans of old used to say: *Divide et impera.*

EZ ordered all recent European attacks: New York 2001, Spain 2004, London 2005, and France 2015. The local secret services executed them obediently.

Collective ingenuousness is the strongest ally of EZ. It makes people always choose the safe side, the politically correct side, the 'least trouble' side; at the time, that makes one feel cowardly, which is a nasty feeling. Hence, collective ingenuousness invented a strategy: always judge the events one by one; avoid considering continuity

60 Children under five were not counted "because they had never known their father anyway".

in history. Then you will always be a *reasonable* coward, which is of course much better than being and unreasonable coward. You end up believing it yourself. Thanks to universal cowardice (it is certainly not an exclusively American trait) EZ gets away with it repeatedly.

What do EZ pull out of their hat in the near future?

- *They will continue the Russian enclosure: after Iraq and Iran, Afghanistan and Ukraine, a whole series of Russian border countries will see their governments destabilized and toppled.*
- *EZ will continue to push for a grand European unification (Great Britain included) in order to facilitate the establishment of a European Federal Bank, modelled on the American one. That is to say, EZ owns that bank, and controls all of Europe.*
- *When after ten years everybody is fed up with the continuous stream of Middle Eastern immigrants who hate everything Europe stands for, EZ will graciously, by mouth of that half-wit Netanyahu, offer to "pacify" Iraq using NATO military equipment. They will do so in less than a week: the time needed to communicate to all EZ fighting squads (ISIS/Daesh, Al-Qaeda, and so forth) that the war is over.*

Ingenuous Patriots, among whom many Christians, will bury EZ under a crashing applause for their extreme efficiency, thus bitterly confirming Our Lord's prophecy:

> The Master commended the dishonest manager for his shrewdness. For the sons of this world are shrewder in dealing with their own generation than the sons of light.[61]

61 Luke 16:8

www.ingramcontent.com/pod-product-compliance
Lightning Source LLC
Chambersburg PA
CBHW050732030426
42336CB00012B/1524

* 9 7 8 1 6 4 5 5 0 4 9 9 3 *